# Aligning Technology with Business for Digital Transformation

# Aligning Technology with Business for Digital Transformation

*Plugging in IT to Light up your Business*

Ashish Pachory

**BEP** BUSINESS EXPERT PRESS

First published in 2020 by
Business Expert Press, LLC
222 East 46th Street, New York, NY 10017
www.businessexpertpress.com

ISBN-13: 978-1-94999-176-5 (paperback)
ISBN-13: 978-1-94999-177-2 (e-book)

Business Expert Press Information Systems Collection

Collection ISSN: 2156-6577 (print)
Collection ISSN: 2156-6593 (electronic)

Cover and interior design by Exeter Premedia Services Private Ltd., Chennai, India

First edition: 2020

10 9 8 7 6 5 4 3 2 1

Printed in the United States of America.

# Abstract

Over the last decade, digital technology has made deep inroads into every walk of life, but perhaps nowhere more than in the world of business. Enterprises must ride the digital wave without losing their grip on the business basics required to stay afloat. Technology now plays an enhanced role in driving business success, creating an entirely new paradigm in which business and technology are inseparable. In this backdrop, business–technology alignment is not a slogan or platitude, but a reality brought upon us by compelling and irreversible changes in our environment.

*Aligning Technology with Business for Digital Transformation* is an intuitive and practical guide to discovering the power of business–technology alignment in the digital era, arguably the most decisive, yet overlooked factor in determining digital enterprise success. Gleaned from decades of experience with global corporations that have shaped the current business–technology landscape, the book covers an indispensable organizational requirement in a simple and relatable way. The basic concepts talked about in the book remind us of the need to seamlessly intertwine new technology with business basics as a sure success formula.

Business–technology alignment is applicable to every member of the digital workforce, as well as those aspiring to become a part of it in the future, and not just the experts and leaders. Hence the book treats the subject in a generic way, focused on orientation rather than specialization. The clearly articulated ideas and insights, relevant examples and stories, and the self-diagnosis tools and exercises presented in the book should, therefore, help not only organizations in unlocking their true potential but also individuals in building the skills and aptitude necessary for succeeding in the digital world.

# Keywords

alignment; aligned to win; business-technology alignment; business-IT alignment; business-IT integration; career; chief information officer; cloud computing; customer experience management; customer lifecycle management; digital business; digital economy; digital education; digital enterprise; digital mindset; digital technology; digital transformation;

digital vision; digital workforce; enterprise mobility; future of work; ICT; information technology; innovation; IT for non-IT; IT services; new-age IT; outcome-based IT; SMAC; technology for business; technology management; transformation

# Contents

# Acknowledgments

One of my hardest decisions yet was to step down from corporate life into the uncharted world of writing, to fulfill an abiding passion. The support and encouragement I received from my family, most notably my mother, Mrs. Madhuri Pachory, and my wife Seema in this difficult transition is invaluable. It is what made this book possible. I, therefore, dedicate it to them with gratitude and pride.

Behind every story and anecdote in this book are people who lent me their time and insights through interviews and survey responses, patiently bearing with my persistence. Without their support, the narrative would have been incomplete, or at best, obscure. I wish I could name all these people individually and express my deep gratitude but am bound by confidentiality.

This book is but a compilation of the ideas, thoughts, experiences, and stories of the many wonderful people with whom I was privileged to share my long professional journey. Many of the life lessons that make up the essence of this book are drawn from these brilliant folks who will never cease to inspire, and to whom I shall be forever indebted.

Writing a book is not a road on which you travel alone. To all who have walked beside me on this exhilarating path, I can only say this: Thank you for being the wind beneath my wings.

# Introduction

Great things happen at intersections. Some of our finest creations are a product of intersecting ideas. Think about it. On its own spoken language was a great idea, but when intersected with the human aptitude for sketching, it gave us writing and thus a way to chronicle information. The rest, of course, is history! The idea of the internal combustion engine when intersected with improved production processes gave us the automobile revolution. Electric power and vapor compression crossed paths to create refrigeration, which, in turn, intersected with shipping to alter the eating habits of people around the world. More recently the intersection of telephony with radio has given us the mobile revolution. Mobile technology has intersected with computer software to place a smart device in our hands that has changed our socializing, banking, and shopping ways forever. It has also replaced many older devices—like camera, video recorder, audio player, calculator, alarm-clock—by further intersecting with advances in micro-miniaturization. The possibilities are limitless.

The magic of intersection has worked in professions too. Through much of history, though, occupations have existed in isolation—often under a religious authority or diktat—unable to realize their combined potential and forge new advancement. This was probably the root cause for the Dark Ages (circa 500 to 1500 AD), a period of human history almost devoid of economic or scientific advancement. *Cross-fertilize or perish* is the clear message to us from our past.

Fortunately, we have learned some lessons from history. We do understand now the value of *collaboration* and *teamwork* in our day-to-day business. For many of us, our careers have been liberally interspersed with pursuits aimed at improving cooperation among cross-functional task forces and teams. There is negligible emphasis on achieving *alignment,* however, since this is assumed to be a derivative of teamwork. As we shall explore in this book, alignment goes much *beyond* teamwork. Let us look at some quick points of difference between teamwork and alignment in Table 0.1.

*Table 0.1 Teamwork and alignment*

|   | **Teamwork** | **Alignment** |
|---|---|---|
| 1 | Driven by common objectives | Guided by shared purpose |
| 2 | Impermanent: Accomplish goal and disband | Permanent: Improves with time |
| 3 | Answers the question, "What are we going to do?" [Examples: Launch cloud-based mobile banking solution in 8 months; shift to new office premises in Quarter 2] | Answers the question, "Who do we intend to be?" [Example: Consistently ahead of the competition in service quality; market leaders in product category X] |
| 4 | Hierarchical structure led by a team leader, where the buck stops. Dedicated formation | Independent of structure or hierarchy. Ownership driven. |

**Example 0.1**

*Many years ago, the senior executives of an IT equipment major convened at their headquarters for the company's annual service meet. On the first day, there were energetic and engaging presentations from the regional service heads to the top management on the accomplishments of their teams toward exceeding their service targets consistently. There was cheer and applause all around, and the chatter around the dinner table later that evening couldn't have been livelier. The next morning, when the conference resumed with an address from the management, a shocking bit of news was broken: the company had not met its customers' service expectations, and this had negatively impacted its financial performance. There was a stunned silence. Disbelief soon yielded to perplexity. How can there be such a disparity between internal measures and customer perception? A lot of deliberation followed, and the root causes were debated. What emerged was that (a) customer service targets were set unilaterally on a one-size-fits-all assumption, (b) measurement was based on factors that customers didn't necessarily care about, like calls per engineer per day, severity-wise call-clearance rate, etc., and (c) there was hardly any communication between the sales (business) and service (technology) functions. This was an instance where all the service units shined independently, but there was no alignment to a shared, larger purpose, leading to organizational failure.*

Let's cut to the present. In the increasingly complex and dynamic business world of today, a company's biggest source of competitive advantage is unquestionably the trust of its customers. Enterprises strive hard to keep their customers happy and loyal, occasionally through some nifty teamwork between the front-end client relationship (business) and the backend service delivery (technology) organizations.

But even as good intentions abound, a *sustained alignment* of business and technology to a common purpose is still at best a platitude. As the digital wave sweeps the world, business–technology alignment can no longer be confined to intentions but emerge as a primary driver of business success.

Let's pause here to get to common ground on the terms "business" and "technology." In this book, business with an upper-case B refers to the Business *organization*, that is, the *people* responsible for presales, sales, marketing, product management, customer relations, business finance, supply chain management (SCM), and other tasks associated with the business function. Technology with an upper-case T refers to the Technology (or IT) *organization*, that is, the *people* responsible for design, development, delivery, operations, service, security, support, and other tasks related to technology products, services, and solutions. Lower-case b or t represents the *discipline* (sphere of activity) of business or technology respectively.

I have introduced the term BITA in this book to refer to Business–Technology Alignment. In most organizations, Technology and IT are overlapping functions, so BITA refers equally to Business–*IT* Alignment.

BITA is a lot more than a pain reliever. As we saw earlier, *intersection is a powerful multiplier of value*. Thus, when business intersects with technology, especially in the digital enterprise context, new possibilities instantly emerge that go far beyond easing existing pain and open new avenues of growth, create and deliver greater value to customers, improve employee engagement, and reduce uncertainty.

Even though technology forms the backbone of business in today's world, very few organizations have done enough to bring Business and Technology together as a strategic force multiplier to drive their growth. Over the years, a lot has changed on both the business and technology dimensions. However, the transactional nature of the Business–Technology relationship has largely remained the same, and a lot of the potential remains locked up.

This book is about discovering the power of BITA and harnessing it for personal and organizational development. It is not a book about technology. The chapters that follow underline the pivotal role played by BITA in your emergence as a successful digital enterprise. The role of IT as an enabler of business evolved over successive IT generations, as presented in Chapter 1. The interdependence of Business and IT in creating business value together is the subject of Chapter 2. In Chapter 3, we consider some of the significant trends in Information and Communication Technology (ICT) and their value as business enablers. Chapter 4 is about the emergence of the digital economy, leading to the creation of the digital enterprise. In Chapter 5, the results of an external survey on the role and importance of BITA in driving business value are presented. An introduction to the seven dimensions of BITA and a tool to calculate your BITA quotient are the subject of Chapter 6. Chapters 7 and 8 are about modeling your digital enterprise, using BITA as the cement to bind its building blocks.

This is the first of two synergistic but independent books on Business–Technology alignment. While this book is a voyage of *discovery* of Business–Technology alignment in your enterprise, the next book in the series, *Mastering the 7 Dimensions of Business–Technology Alignment*, provides simple techniques for the *conquest* of its seven dimensions.

The emphasis in both books is on building and sustaining close alignment between Business and Technology. However, healthy functional alignment between other parts of the organization, for example, business and human resources (HR), or IT and supply chain management (SCM) is also relevant in the current business context and many of the principles in both books apply to these as well.

As the purpose of this book is not to teach but to awaken, it steers clear of arcane concepts that may seem exalted but lack practical appeal. Therefore, most ideas in this book will have a ring of familiarity, and that is by design. Quite like quality and customer focus, BITA is all about excellence orientation, which this book will guide you to discover and develop.

# CHAPTER 1

# The Way Things Were...

The universe, they say, started with a Big Bang and went through a phase of hyperinflationary growth before things cooled down and the expansion rate stabilized. Once this happened, conditions evolved that produced stars, planets, life (at least here on Earth), and eventually, pockets of *intelligence*.

As it morphed into its present form, the universe also splintered into *dimensions*. There was no concept of space and time before the creation event. Don't get alarmed yet—this is not a book on the physics of the Big Bang! The reason I bring up the subject in the opening lines is that the universe is the best model to explain the concept of hyperinflationary growth along *multiple dimensions*. As we shall see in later chapters, the concept of dimensions has a special significance for Business–IT alignment.

Let's turn to Information Technology. Unlike the universe, Information Technology did not have very spectacular origins. There was no Big Bang. Information processing systems arrived on the scene around the middle of the twentieth century in successive stages. It was, however, not until the 1980s that computing and networking technology scaled up sufficiently to make computers accessible (easy-to-use) and feasible (fit-to-use) in the business environment. This intersection of technology with business released a continuous wave of evolution and adoption, which drove not just the growth of IT, but created, ultimately, an entirely new paradigm in which IT became inseparable from Business.

We will return to this subject, but for now, let us go back to the origins of IT and the way things were for the Business–IT ecosystem. While the first computer, called ENIAC, arrived in 1946 it would be inaccurate to say that it spawned an IT revolution. Continuous advancements led to computers finally emerging from highly specialized, dedicated, and often secret environments into the public domain on a time-share basis. IBM System 360 mainframe computer was a groundbreaking step in facilitating this movement as it heralded a shift from discrete transistors and relays to *integrated circuits* and a *scalable architecture*, forming the foundation for *digital computing*. CDC, DEC, HP, and others followed with their versions, and by about the early to mid-1970s, several scientific institutions and business corporations were relying on mainframe computers for input, output, storage, and processing of data. The sturdy mainframe remained well entrenched in our business, educational, financial, and research institutions at least up to the mid-1980s. These mainframes were sturdy machines built for bulk processing, but their display, retrieval, and information-sharing capabilities were quite limited, so *printing* was very central to computing.

The IT story is marked by significant and frequent generational shifts, driven by new technology. With each generation, things became simpler for the user, thus increasing the rate of *adoption*. Up to about 1980, there was a specialized group of people, notably computer engineers, scientists, and programmers, who alone could lay claim to knowledge of IT and its limited applications. Look where we are now with the adoption of IT. The story of the *evolution* of technology, helped by Moore's law, is similar. What took a room full of hardware then, comfortably fits into your pocket now! This steady growth in technological evolution and the rate of adoption thus takes the form of an ice-cream cone when plotted on a timescale (Figure 1.1).

Many of us in our lifetimes have seen IT evolve from *Mainframes* to *Mini-computers* (mid-range batch-processing systems) to *Client-Server* architecture to *Internet* to *Cloud computing*. That is five generations of IT in one of ours! With the spawning of each new generation, the realization that IT can play a larger role than "keeping the light-bulb on" became further ingrained.

IT's potential in the organization enlarged over the generations from an instrument of automation to a tool for productivity, and finally, an enabler of business. We are concerned in this book primarily with the emergence of IT as a business enabler. This happened around the fourth generation of IT.

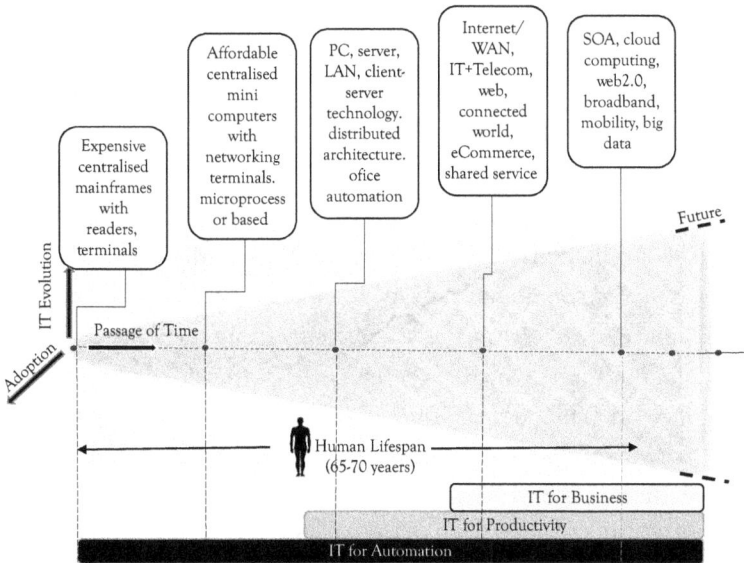

*Figure 1.1 IT evolution and adoption*

In the early generations, the picture was starkly different from what we see today. Actually, there was no picture at all, as IT was completely invisible to all but itself. An IT (or EDP, which stands for Electronic Data Processing, as it was then called) *department* was where data was keyed-in manually from vouchers on to diskettes, which were fed into batch-processing computers running COBOL programs, with programmers within shouting distance always! In the background used to be boisterous line printers, always printing away on reams of lined paper. To this day, I wonder who consumed those reports and why! Then Y2K, the biggest damp squib in recorded history, happened and people woke up to the existence of IT, though no one was quite sure of its role in their lives.

In the above scenario, Business and IT existed in completely different, non-intersecting universes. The advent of PCs and rudimentary LAN made a case for IT to be seen (though still not heard) around the office. Even as IT was gaining some acceptance as an enhancer of office productivity in the early 1980s, it was still not in the realm of being a real *business enabler*. Business–IT Alignment was beyond even the remote reaches of imagination in those times.

Things started changing rather swiftly with the arrival of the public Internet around 1983. The operating word here is public, for the Internet had existed in a limited way since the late 1960s when the U.S. Advanced Research Projects Agency (ARPA) interconnected some university computers and created the first-ever *network* of computers, called ARPANET. The ARPANET served the interests of scientific users only and had limited extent. However, it was the earliest demonstration of *packet-based* communication, which means sending information in small units over different paths and reconstructing the units at the destination. This formed the basis of the TCP/IP (which is an acronym for the somewhat grandiloquent *Transport Control Protocol over Internet Protocol*, but you can ignore this. Just call it *packet transfer*), which allowed for orderly expansion to include more and more computers in the network. TCP/IP became the lifeline of what we now know as the Internet and is still used as the dominant protocol for Internet communication.

Two other things happened in the early 1980s that brought the Internet into the public arena. One, the creation of the World Wide Web enabling sharing of information (pages) over a TCP/IP network and two, the introduction of the *web browser*.

An understanding of the state of Business–Technology relationship in the *pre-Internet era* is an integral part of appreciating the power of Business–IT Alignment (BITA). For far too long, IT systems operated invisibly, run by the EDP staff. The other genre associated with IT was the computer scientist—the erudite product of a top technological institute whose work was mostly confined to research on how to build better computers and not on how to make better use of computers for business. Hence, most of these scientists went to work for technology firms, usually manufacturers of computer equipment, and not EDP.

In this scenario, most companies had no means to see beyond the usual invoice printing, management information system (MIS), and other routine batch-processing jobs performed by *minicomputers* (as per today's standards they were mini in everything but size!) and there was very little attempt to exploit the power of computers for anything beyond mechanization of existing—mostly financial—processes. The following is an example from that era.

**Example 1.1**

*A former colleague, presently a Vice-President with an IT infrastructure company in the United States, recalled this incident from 1984, when he was an IT maintenance engineer for minicomputer systems in Delhi, India. On getting a call from a customer—a textile yarn mill about 80 km outside Delhi—on a Saturday morning, he rushed to the site by bus. On arriving at the site, he was told by a flustered EDP manager that on the previous day (Friday), an urgent meeting had taken place between the company's sales managers and the Finance Head, which ended with the decision to implement a new product-coding system for reporting itemized sales. It was further agreed that this would be the high point of the meeting with the managing director during his forthcoming visit next Tuesday (yes, three days later), where the sales based on the new categories would be presented for the first time.*

*There was no one from IT (EDP) present during that Friday meeting. However, it was cheerily stated by the Finance Head that "we have a computer, so we can easily do it. After all, what are computers for?" Now, these product codes were embedded in a variety of datasets, from material receipt notes to customer invoices. The change would need to be run on volumes of records stored on countless time-consuming tapes. With all the smart scripting that my friend and the EDP team tried, the job could not be done, and the EDP manager had the unpleasant task on Monday evening to ask for an additional 14 days from his boss, the Finance Head. My friend was told later that the meeting with the Managing Director on Tuesday did not go well for the Finance Head and commitments on some new product launches were slipped, which probably affected revenues and disconcerted the sales folks as well. It took days to recover from the effects of one wrong communication that could have been avoided had there been some alignment with IT either before or during a crucial meeting. But such instances were commonplace as IT did not merit a say on critical decisions that it was asked to implement.*

As evident from this example, IT was only a backend tool for *automation*. Nothing more. It had no place in decision making. There was also no attempt to use IT for any optimization or improvement of processes. Even the accuracy of calculations was doubted—I have seen folks sitting with computer-generated reports, verifying totals on a calculator!

To be fair, the minicomputer had its limitations as an enabler of Business–IT interface. It was a batch processing system that relied on data fed through offline data entry machines. There was no "non-IT" interface envisaged in its construction. As seems quite inevitable in retrospect, it soon yielded to another exciting development in the early 1980s—the arrival of the Personal Computer, or simply the PC, introduced by IBM and later cloned by others. The PC filled a very significant gap, as it heralded the use of computers for rudimentary business purpose, *directly by the end user*. The computer had finally broken out of the lab and the EDP department.

The early business use, of course, was mostly limited to word processing and spreadsheets. While it was indeed a boost for individual *productivity*, computers and IT were still very far from being enablers of business in the real world, and the concept of Business–IT alignment was entirely alien. It was an era in which the device defined the landscape of IT and trumped data and applications. Still, the computer age had now firmly arrived. It was uncannily prophetic of *Time* magazine to break tradition and declare the PC, a machine, as its *person of the year* in 1983!

The PC helped usher in another very significant development. For the first time, people could transfer their data to *another* computer, by *saving* it on the humble floppy disk with its limited (1.2 MB) capacity. (Notice that the "Save" icon on many applications, like Word, is still in the shape of a floppy disk!) Theoretically, data transfer was possible between mainframes and minicomputers as well, but as there was no *universal operating system* that different computers could understand, it was restricted to very tight, allied groups. The sharing of data between disjoint computers (PCs) was largely possible with the arrival of Microsoft on the scene with its Disk Operating System (MS-DOS). MS-DOS soon became a standard platform for PCs, allowing portable applications for the first time, thus revolutionizing the way people used computers. So, did everyone now rush to hop on to the IT bandwagon? Not by a long shot, unfortunately.

**Example 1.2**

*IT was still considered an expensive indulgence by most institutions in the 1980s. Protests against computerization were common. There was very little understanding of the gain that the computer could bring, and most of the contemplation was around the perceived pain it entailed. Far from being an enabler of business success, the PC was seen as an avoidable extravagance and a threat to job security. I was in Lucknow (India) in 1985 to meet with the head of a renowned scientific institution—a very learned man, well-grounded but with eyes to the sky. His problem was that despite having used his available grant to have high-end personal computers installed in his institute, he was unable to convince his team of scientists and research associates to use those computers, which would justify the investment. On probing, it emerged that using the PCs for the work would result in some of the on going programs finishing much ahead of schedule, which was not desirable since the stipend of the lab staff was linked to the duration of the project! Clearly, this was a problem that was not envisaged at the time of the business-case preparation! I was asked to join his staff meeting that day, to convince the team of the benefits of using computers, as an outside "expert." Incredible as it may seem, we could not succeed, and the project went ahead without using the computers though there was some agreement that future programs would factor-in the use of computers after due training was provided. I could only convince the team to use the machines for some required documentation, making the storage, retrieval, and editing process more manageable. This case highlights the state of affairs even in relatively very learned communities of those times. Attitudes and mindsets were not aligned with the ready adoption of technology.*

Stances toward the adoption of technology for business started becoming more favorable with the advent of the *client–server* model of computing. The client–server architecture heralded a new era, which would eventually spawn many of the services (like E-mail, web) that contribute to Business–IT alignment.

*Clients* are applications that rely on servers for processing power. *Servers* are centralized processing systems that manage all the resources like files and data, and execute all the process requests from the clients, while the *network* connects the servers and clients so that they can communicate and share information.

As *microcomputers* (PCs) became more affordable and increasingly powerful, protocols evolved to interconnect them and *share* their combined computing power. This gave rise to the *Local Area Network*, which is an extensible system of interconnected computers communicating through a well-defined protocol, permitting seamless expansion. In this system of interconnected computers (computers are called *hosts* in networking terminology), any individual computer could play the role of *either* a server *or* a client or *both*. A client or server could be an *application* (and not necessarily a computer), running on a host. The e-mail that you routinely use is an excellent example of a *client* as it enables you to send messages to an unseen mail *server*, which processes the message to decide on further action, like forwarding it to its intended destination client.

The client–server architecture is an important milestone in the evolution of the Internet. The Internet is merely a vast network of interconnected hosts (running as clients *or* servers) communicating via a defined protocol (TCP/IP) for sharing information (web pages) using client–server architecture.

We have come a long way from the days of the IBM 360. Today we have a vibrant Internet, which encompasses diverse developments in computing architecture, communication networks, devices, and software, which happened independently of each other. The Internet is a living demonstration of the power of intersection.

We come across mind-boggling statistics on Internet adoption every day, and on its innovative use in social, business, scientific, educational, and other human endeavors. Now, in fact, the Internet has gone beyond human consumption and is making fast strides into the realm of *Things*, opening the road to smart cities and beyond! As far as technology is concerned, the Internet may be just another example of what successive intersections of ideas can achieve, but for business, it unveils completely new vistas that call for a quick rebooting of the very fundamentals of trade, customer management, and go-to-market. It is survival. In the Internet world, Business and IT *together* create business value. They do not just complement each other. They are inseparable.

There's a lot more to the Internet story. Connectivity has become ubiquitous, and it no longer matters whether you are using your office laptop, your personal smartphone, or your friend's borrowed tablet. You are no longer restricted in your access to your private or business data and applications by your location or device because your content (data, applications) can now reside on a remote *Cloud* instead of locally on a device. This imparts *Mobility* (freedom), another new trend spawned by the Internet, which, along with the Cloud, has had a profound impact on the social and business landscape. The next generation of the World Wide Web is already on its way. Web 2.0 will increase the scope for online collaboration and provide better structure and organization of content.

The Internet saga continues. To accommodate more users (which would now include "things" or "machines"), the current *addressing system* is being revamped. An address refers to the unique identity of a device on the network. As the Internet is based on a binary (i.e., base of 2) system, the current 32-bit addressing protocol, known as IPv4, can identify up to $2^{32}$, or 4.3 billion users. This is grossly inadequate, considering the proliferation of connected devices, including *things*. The *new* addressing system (IPv6) would use *128*-bits! By the way, this is not just four times increase in capacity, but a staggering $2^{96}$ times (which is around 72 billion billion billion times)! IPv6 would hold out even if every particle in the known universe were to have its own IP address!

This chapter has been a rather breezy journey through the various stages of IT evolution and adoption. It is intended to help us gain an understanding of the way things were, as a precursor to defining the way things are in the new Business–IT ecosystem. Business and IT have become inseparably intertwined by the web and its progeny. The opportunities for both Business and IT in this environment are limitless. However, making the most of these opportunities requires a conscious effort on the part of both Business and IT participants. They must be *aligned* to a common purpose, and this is what we shall be discussing in the rest of this book.

# CHAPTER 2

# Business–IT Alignment: Platitude or Survival?

If you are still in an organization where the alignment of IT with Business is a mere platitude, let me offer this advice to you: Get off the bus before it tumbles down the ravine. Business—IT alignment (BITA) is not another well-tossed transformation brew stirred up by hype rather than value. It is a ground-up reality brought upon us by compelling and irreversible changes in our environment — market, economic, social, and of course, technological. It is survival.

We saw in the previous chapter that for most of their history, Business and IT existed in completely different, nonintersecting universes. Let us cut to the present. The amalgamation of IP-centric technologies, an abundance of bandwidth, explosion of data, the proliferation of smart mobile devices, and a growing hunger for actionable information anywhere and anytime, have resulted in the creation of the new-age digital ecosystem, which has turned all traditional concepts on their heads. The foundation of the integrated business–technology edifice of the future has been laid. Alignment of technology with business in this backdrop is not about platitudes or catchy slogans, or even mission statements. It is about Technology and Business thinking, building and operating *together* for a shared goal, and that is to make the business successful. If this simple tenet is demonstrated in the day-to-day behavior of the workforce, you have already taken a significant first step toward alignment of technology with business. For the new-age digital enterprise, this must become the new normal.

We will return to the new normal in a moment, but first, let us be clear about "the demonstration of day-to-day *behavior*" since this is at the very root of BITA. Quite like customer orientation and quality focus, BITA is part of the organization's *character*. It cannot be attained unless

everyone in Business and Technology is passionate about their responsibility toward the achievement of *organizational* (and not only depart-
mental) success and feel connected to the larger mission of the company.
BITA can never truly happen as a response to a directive, or compliance
with a policy. It must be a voice from *within* which makes you act it out
instinctively and naturally.

The following true cases have nothing to do with technology and not
much to do with business either, but they are a great demonstration of
*intrinsic behavior*, which collectively builds organizational character:

(a) A teller at a public sector bank in Delhi gets a call from an ordi-
nary customer about an urgent need of cash to meet an emergency.
The customer cannot come to the bank as she has a six-month old
infant to look after. It is 112°F outside, with dusty winds blowing
that could give one a stroke. The teller braves the weather on his two-
wheeler scooter to deliver the cash at home and collect the cheque,
going beyond his charter.

(b) A taxi driver tracks down a passenger who had left behind the
engagement ring that the passenger was to present to his fiancée that
very day. He made the deliverance of the ring a priority over getting
more passengers, understanding the role that the ring played in the
happiness of two people.

(c) When New Zealand's Nikki Hamblin tripped and fell during the
5,000 m heats at the Rio Olympics, Abbey D'Agostino of the United
States sacrifices her race and turns around to help the prone New
Zealander, in a true demonstration of sportsmanship.

(d) A sales manager says a firm no to his prospective customer's request
for a arranging and paying for a hired car to ferry the customer's
personal guests to a hill resort, as a token of his "appreciation" of
the customer's order, because it would have been out-of-line with
his company's and personal ethics code, even at the risk of losing a
hard-fought deal, which would earn him a handsome bonus. There
was never even any doubt or question about it.

(e) When Oscar Munoz, CEO of United, while waiting to board a flight
at a Florida airport, chats up with a nervous old lady next to him who
confided that she had rarely ever flown and was terrified of crowded

planes. When she entered the plane, Oscar offered her his first-class seat, making her experience one to remember for the right reasons!

Even as technology becomes increasingly dominant in influencing business outcomes, demonstrating behaviors that reflect values, work ethics, and resolve will always be a factor in defining excellence, as exemplified in the above stories, and in many others that I am sure you can relate from your own experiences. Likewise, BITA is an *intrinsic* part of professional excellence that cannot be supplanted through policies and directives, nor is it open to compromise. This is why "demonstrating day-to-day behavior" that we referred to earlier is so important in the context of BITA.

What individuals in a group consciously, consistently, and collectively demonstrate in their behavior becomes its culture. It is true of all communities, including business corporations. This is the reason that excellent companies have belief systems, which is an *unchanging* set of behaviors—for example, serving the customer well, conducting business ethically, setting high standards of quality, and so on—that every employee is expected to emulate in word and spirit. It's the belief system, shared by all the employees, that builds the *culture* of the organization. An organization has *character* when it does not compromise on its belief system irrespective of inducements, compulsions, or consequences. For Business and IT to succeed together consistently, BITA must be ingrained in the organization's belief system and reflect in its culture *and* character.

How do you inculcate a strong belief system across the length and breadth of the organization? As this is driven by a *shared passion,* there is no standard formula here, but a few pointers could be useful:

- The leadership of the company reinforces the belief system by living it, commenting on it, measuring it, and communicating it at every opportunity.
- The leadership always decides in favor of the belief system during organizational crises. Their reactions are guided by the belief system, and they act as role-models for the organization.
- It is made mandatory for every person in the organization to participate at least annually in coaching sessions *by the leadership itself* to reinforce the belief system.

- The company's rewards and recognition programs are modeled on the belief system.
- Respecting the belief system forms an important and uncompromising criterion for recruitment, performance assessments, and progression.

## Outcome-Based IT

Let us return now to the new normal. In the current digitally charged environment, Business and IT are no longer isolated entities driven by functional objectives. Instead, they are bound together by the *shared mission* of making the business successful.

In other words, the new normal is about IT being an equal stakeholder in the achievement of business results, or *outcomes*. IT is no longer just an emergency-response team to cater to outages and issues. The true measure of IT's performance is the impact it has on the *outcome* of *business processes*. Internal measures like efficiency and productivity of IT resources are, therefore, no longer useful indicators of business value. Outcome-based IT is focused on *what* was achieved, rather than *how* it was achieved. Being focused on the same outcome indicates a *common purpose*, which is at the core of any alignment. *The outcome-based model of IT is thus the essence of BITA.*

The good news is that outcome-based IT has quickly come to a point where it is well entrenched in business. Consider these examples.

**Manufacturing:** Traditionally, IT has been tasked with the automation of the process workflow in a manufacturing environment while the actual outcome of those processes is the shop-floor users' responsibility. In the outcome-based model, the role of IT would be achieving just-in-time (JIT) manufacturing and lean production to reduce cost (a *business* outcome).

**Banking:** IT is now a primary stakeholder in the growth of the banking business through the enablement of Internet and mobile banking, and adapting quickly to changing customer preferences. For example, in the outcome-based model, IT would be responsible for ensuring the speed of fund transfers, security of online banking transactions, simplicity of user experience, and so on.

**Telecom:** In high-tech sectors like telecom, IT has an even higher influence on the business outcome, as a leading light to the Business in *proposing* innovative solutions in areas like monetization of data and business analytics. The primary *business* outcomes like rapid customer acquisition and accuracy of billing are measures of IT success in the outcome-based model. The outcome of many of the new telecom services like mobile payments is dependent on a healthy BITA. This trend is likely to only increase, especially with the mainstreaming of many over-the-top services.

**Airlines:** The speed and convenience with which you can book an airline ticket while on the move is an example of BITA at work in an outcome-driven model. The ease and precision with which an airline can offer seat selection, meal preferences, flight status, check-ins, discounts, and loyalty programs to its customers are also a measure of IT's contribution to the achievement of business outcomes—in this case getting you airborne comfortably, conveniently, and cost-effectively. Conversely, is IT accountable for the dwindling loyalty of the airline's customer base? In the outcome-based model, it most certainly is.

In all the above scenarios, any discussion on the uptime of an IT server, or first-call-effectiveness (FCE) of an IT engineer, or rate of central processing unit (CPU) utilization would be at best an academic one! Frankly, no one cares. All that matters is how well IT has been able to contribute to the success of the business and its stakeholders. In short, the *business outcome* of IT. This trend is not likely to abate down the road.

---

**Example 2.1**

*A global leader in high-tech medical equipment organized its annual Asia-Pacific (APAC) service conclave in Singapore. The theme of the conclave was "service strategy as a market differentiator," a novel idea for those times (it was 1999)! Presentations on service strategy were made by the service managers from 12 participating countries. The delegates were mildly surprised to see not one but two people stepping up for the presentation by one of the participant countries. It turned out that one was the service manager while the other was the sales manager. Why the sales manager? This was, after all, a service conference! It was not very common to see sales and service folks on one stage! The audience's curiosity was soon satiated. It had so happened that a few months ago, there was a frantic call from the operator of the MRI scanner machine at a hospital-cum-research facility to the company's salesperson, who had sold the equipment to the hospital. The hospital's worst nightmare had come true. There was an unconscious patient whose magnetic scan was being done for which he had been placed on the sliding table and pushed into the tubular scanner. Due to some glitch, it wouldn't retract and open, locking the patient inside! The patient being unconscious could not operate the emergency button inside. The machine had a console from where the operator ran it, but he only saw a flashing error message when he tried retracting. The operator did not even have the service engineer's phone number and instead called the sales guy, as it was the only number he had. On hearing the story, the sales guy also tensed up and imme-diately reached the service engineer for help. The engineer instantly left for the hospital, but would he make it in time? Probably because of a time-out mechanism (which no one knew about), the machine opened on its own after a few taut minutes, and the patient was saved! But it imparted some crucial lessons. First, the service (Technology) team was measuring itself on parameters that did not factor-in catastrophic situations like the above. The focus was clearly internal and not on the* outcome, *which in this case was ensuring the safety of the patient while providing accurate diagnostics. Second, there was no interaction between sales and service to plan an emergency response along with the hospi-tal (customer) teams, like building a remote control-center manned by technical experts, on-site IT availability, and so on (all focused on the outcome). The good thing was that after this incident, the company's management decided that sales and service teams would henceforth cre-ate their strategy and operations plans jointly and communicate them to the world together. That is, be equal stakeholders. Which is why the sales and service managers were together on the stage, presenting the service strategy. A big round of applause followed! A good lesson learned the hard way. Though most of the folks present did not recognize it then, this was probably their first introduction to the importance of outcome-based IT.*

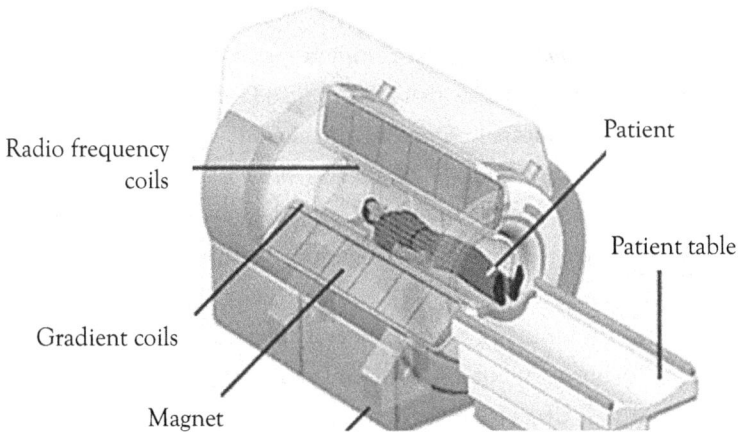

Radio frequency coils

Patient

Patient table

Gradient coils

Magnet

*Figure 2.1  MRI scanner*

For true and sustained alignment that goes beyond platitudes and slogans, there must be strong *interdependency* between Business and IT. They can no longer afford to be in different universes.

So, what do companies that have strong BITA in their DNA, and are therefore driven by the outcome-based model of IT, do *differently*? Let us look at a few examples of behaviors that are commonly displayed in almost all companies where BITA is a lot more than a platitude or slogan.

1. *Business and IT operate as two-in-a-box.* There are no boundaries between Business and IT as viewed by the customer. Business and IT are equal partners in customer value creation, presenting a seamless customer interface. This requires constant formal and informal communication between Business and IT to stay in sync throughout the customer lifecycle.

2. *The IT organization is business-led.* This means that there are empowered business champions for each business unit within the IT organization, with the responsibility and authority to keep IT priorities tuned to business requirements.

3. IT team works as a *thought leader to the business team*, rather than an order taker. As domain experts, the IT organization must be a trusted advisor to the business, providing thought-leading insights on trends and technologies that help the business succeed.

4. *The IT strategy and architecture are continually evaluated against the business roadmap.* The most common reason for misalignment is a divergence in strategies that lead to an IT architecture that is not supportive of future business requirements.

5. *It is business that drives the IT processes and not the other way!* IT processes are painless and straightforward, designed to *serve the needs of the business*. All processes are dynamic and adaptable to the changing business climate.

6. It is typical for the IT team to be evaluated not only on the benefits of IT to business, but also the *costs* (monetary and nonmonetary) at which these benefits are delivered. This is best indicated by *Business and IT regularly monitoring and reviewing the* business value of IT (BVIT).[1]

7. IT is business funded and hence, Business is a stakeholder in IT and has a strong vote in prioritizing IT investments. Models are in place to measure IT consumption by each business unit and to tie back the business benefits of a solution to the investment made in its roll out.

Attainment of strong BITA calls for several concerted and well-thought-out actions on the part of both Business and IT. As a first step, we need to establish our current bearings, that is, ascertain our strengths and improvement areas. The BITA tool introduced later in this book (Chapter 6) is one of the means to do this. This tool is also available on www.alignedtowin.com, so that it may be easily personalized for your environment.

Here is an example of how alignment, even an enforced one, can be a savior in sticky situations.

---

**Example 2.2**

*We were executing a major business transformation project with a leading telecom service provider in the Asia Pacific. The project revolved around building the billing and charging platform and was highly time-bound. The customer's ability to launch new services in the market hinged strongly on the on-time availability of this system. There were many parties involved—the customer's own IT team, billing product vendor, system integrator (my team), and a few other smaller suppliers of adjunct products. Six months into the project, we were slipping milestones and anticipated a major derailment that would take us a year or more from the original plan. The project was led by the astute Chief Information Officer (CIO) of the customer's organization, who fully understood that the situation called for some drastic steps as missing the business commitment was out of the question. I heard with dismay the presentation from the senior executive of the product company, whose pitch was on one aspect only—that projects of this magnitude are universally delayed, so there was nothing unique in this situation. And hence, "don't worry," was his guidance, "your management will understand"! There was no counsel from him on how the project could be herded back on track.*

*Word reached the customer's CEO and he called an all-hands meeting. There was a great deal of censure and reprimand, but more disturbingly, there was a visible disappointment on the CEO's face. He even reproached his CIO and the team. Finally, he said that what was clearly missing was an alignment between the various teams involved, particularly with the Business, thereby eroding the urgency around the project which he expected to see. It seemed that no one was accountable, and the CIO was being pulled in too many directions. The meeting ended with an agreement among the stakeholder on a few decisive actions:*

1. *Any delay in billing to end-customers will be the accountability of the IT team, who will, if required, do the billing offline starting from the scheduled cut-over date.*
2. *The Business team will have two empowered representatives permanently assigned to this project, with authority to take decisions on all matters impacting the project. Issues will be dealt with as and when they surfaced.*
3. *The business team was also brought onboard on a phased approach and scope-freeze.*
4. *All future change requirements will be funded from the business budget and not from the already stretched project budget.*

> 5. *Lastly, the CEO asked that a weekly progress update be given to him face-to-face, with very solid reasons given for any slippage. He set aside 30 minutes each week for this review.*
>
> *A new baseline was created and agreed with Business. The sense of urgency was palpable. We ended up taking the project phases into production on schedule. Confidence grew in the collaboration, and another key transformation project is underway with the same constitution of partners. Such is the power of BITA, even if it was an enforced one in this instance.*

Many organizations follow the concept of Business being an *internal customer* to IT. While this is fine for *the shared-services* model, which is typically driven by a service level agreement (SLA) and not by business outcome, the internal customer concept does not work best for BITA. An internal customer approach often causes confusion about who is the real customer and imparts—to the IT team—a feeling of being one layer removed from the end customer. The customer always means the end-user, who pays for your services or products. Remember this: In a BITA-driven organization, everyone in IT and Business is a *Customer Satisfier,* and that is the *only* role they play. It does not matter what their calling cards proclaim.

The outcome-driven model follows a cycle in which both Business and IT are participants. They are fully aligned in their view of the desired outcome early in the cycle. That is, both Business and IT have a clear and well-coordinated plan to achieve the outcome as a shared mission. *Unless Business and IT are aligned early in the game on the need and the desirability of an action, there will never be alignment on the* outcome.

In an outcome-based model, the relationship between Business and IT goes beyond the traditional requirements sign-off to a shared ownership of the outcome and its impact on the business. Hence it is vital that they *both* answer "Yes" to *all* the questions in the cycle (Figure 2.2). In this case, we have considered the launch of a Mobile Self-Service portal, but the surrounding questions apply equally to all ventures, including changes that may arise in the course of a venture. Always test your alignment *early in the game* through clear agreement on the answers.

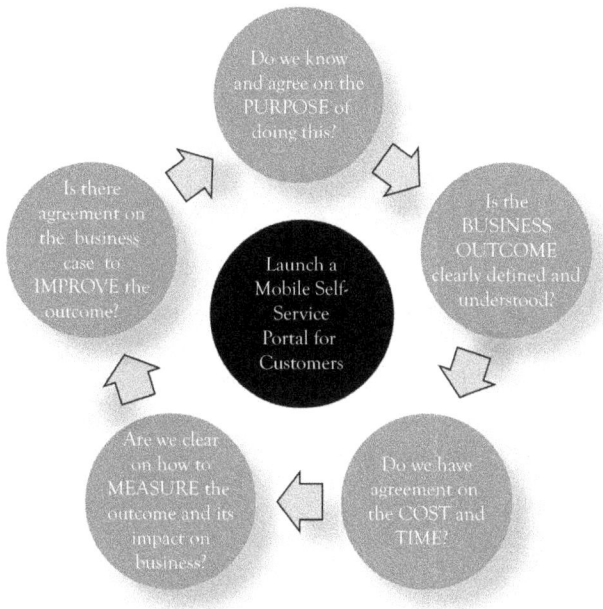

*Figure 2.2* **A test for alignment**

In summary, (1) defining the outcome must be the *starting point* of an engagement and not a corollary, and (2) the outcome must be commonly understood and owned by both Business and IT.

There is no organized industry today where IT does not have a role in shaping the product that reaches the end customer. In such a scenario, imagine for a moment that Business and IT are *not* aligned, and are still in the state of 1980s and 1990s described in the previous chapter. It is not just that chaos will ensue, which it inevitably will. More to the point, Business—which survived even Y2K—will come to a grinding halt. IT is at the very *core* of business today. In fact, it is indistinguishable from Business. For the new-age enterprise, Business *is* IT. And vice-versa.

## The Cycle of Interdependence

The cycle of interdependence, as depicted in Figure 2.3, is at the core of BITA. In an organization where Business and IT are truly aligned, they are also interdependent. Let us look briefly at some of the elements that are at the heart of this interdependence and how they influence BITA:

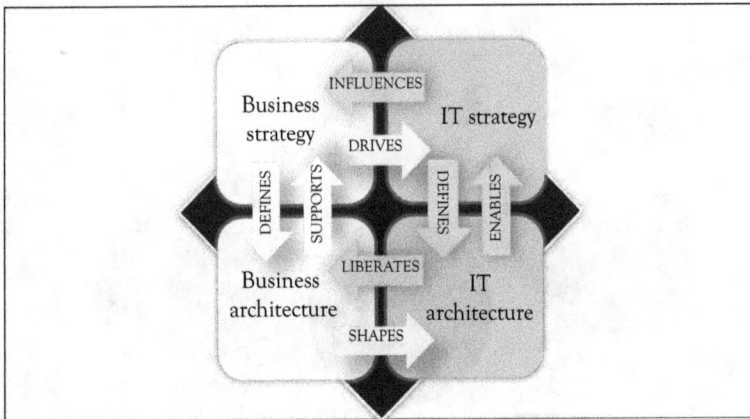

*Figure 2.3 Cycle of interdependence*

- The Business strategy lays the foundation for the IT strategy. One of the defining characteristics of BITA-led organizations is that their IT strategy flows down from a very clear and uncomplicated charter: *IT exists to make the business succeed.* Period. Hence the IT strategy must ensure that two objectives are met. First, IT is aligned with the business roadmap, that is, IT organization, systems, and processes can effectively and efficiently support, enable, and execute the company's *business* plan. Second, IT transformation is a continuous process, that is, IT service delivery and application architecture are continuously *evolving* to keep up with the dynamic business environment.

- The IT architecture must be defined by the IT strategy (which in turn is determined by the Business strategy, as we saw). A lot of organizations find themselves constrained by their IT architecture, which over the years has become clunky and patchy. They have no option but to allow the architecture to influence their strategy, which is a gross mistake. In the fast-changing technology scenario, your IT architecture may be the biggest constraint in delivering those mobility-driven (cloud-enabled) services that your customer expects, and your competitor is already providing. In a BITA-driven organization, the IT architecture is built-for-the-future. It is based on standards which provide for modularity and scalability so that the architecture can keep in lockstep with the evolving strategy.

- In the digital world where business outcomes are increasingly dependent on IT, a business strategy is also increasingly *influenced* by the IT strategy. A business strategy cannot by itself drive business success in the current technology-driven environment. The Business, therefore, must factor in the IT capabilities and roadmap to arrive at a winning strategy. Both Business and IT understand that to win in the market, differentiation is the key, and this differentiation rides very heavily on Business and IT having a converged strategy.

- A word on the Business architecture, which is part of the cycle of interdependence. The Business architecture is what enables organizations to visualize their business *as a whole*, rather than as small pieces that somehow fit together. It is a description of the structure and interaction between the business strategy, organization, functions, processes, and information needs. In short, business architecture is the *blueprint* for aligning the organization with its mission and forms the bridge between a company's business strategy and its successful execution ("how to?"). In organizations with strong BITA, the IT architecture can truly liberate the business architecture by incrementally transforming and adapting itself to the changing needs of the business. For example, the ease and alacrity with which an organization can perform its business process reengineering, considering that most process workflows are IT-enabled, would be a good indicator of the liberating effect of the IT architecture on the Business architecture.

- The IT architecture is among the most influential factors for sustaining a strong BITA in the enterprise. A nonsupportive IT architecture is a constraint to new business offerings. On the other hand, a modular and scalable architecture enables a quick, efficient, and seamless launch of new services, which is part of any good IT strategy. To support a dynamic IT strategy, *Enterprise Architecture (EA)*, which is a conceptual blueprint that defines how technology benefits and serves the organization's current and future business objectives, is most effective from a BITA perspective.

While going into a detailed study of EA methodology would lead us into technical territory, which may fall outside the comfort zone of many of us, it may nevertheless be useful to touch upon the role of an EA framework, such as The Open Group Architecture Framework (TOGAF). TOGAF helps align IT architecture objectives with business goals for quick and efficient delivery of IT services, by systematically organizing IT delivery process to achieve close alignment of IT with Business.[3]

The reason TOGAF blends seamlessly with BITA is that it enables enterprises to implement technology solutions in a structured and organized way, with a focus on meeting business objectives. This means that it allows IT-related services (e.g., business applications) to be added, removed, and modified quickly without impacting the base architecture, or the platform, which consists of all the standard and reusable services. Interested readers may like to visit The Open Group website www.open-group.org/togaf for a detailed study of TOGAF.

The short of the story is that an elegant and standard IT architecture, like EA, is highly conducive to BITA as it enables IT to launch new and differentiated business services seamlessly and effortlessly.

A lot of people have asked me, "What's your IT strategy?" My answer to this question is always the same: IT exists to make the business succeed. The best strategy for IT is, therefore, to harmonize the IT people, processes, and systems with the *business* goals so that IT's success is a function of business success. You cannot have a secure cabin on a sinking ship, or an IT that is successful while the business is a failure.

A strategy is nothing but a plan to achieve the mission of the company. Business and IT are constituents of a larger entity—the organization—guided by the same mission. Hence the IT strategy and business strategy must be fully convergent. The template for the IT strategy is already available in the form of the business strategy, and IT just need to conform to this.

Business-outcome based IT has obvious implications on the organization and its people too. Business people are now required to be tech-savvy, and IT people are required to be business savvy. There must be a correlation in the key result areas (KRAs) of Business and IT teams. Indeed, IT organizations are now emphasizing business-mindedness in hiring for technical roles. Lines are blurring. We may soon see more business managers becoming CIOs and CIOs becoming CEOs. In most business-aligned IT organizations, the core IT team is a group of influencers, serving as navigators and facilitators toward accomplishing the business mission. Typically, all routine operations are outsourced to like-minded partners. This trend helps in directing the organization's energies to its core strategic areas and is insulation against technological upheavals requiring new skill-sets in large numbers.

BITA is certainly not a platitude in today's tech-dominated business world. It is a *requisite* for the business to succeed today. However, it is not a trivial task and should not be underestimated. Organizations must consciously and consistently strive to achieve it.

At this point, let us take a quick guided tour of the new world of IT, which is vastly different from the one we came across in Chapter 1. Here, IT does not just influence the business, but *shapes* it, as we shall see in the next chapter.

# CHAPTER 3

# The Way Things Are ...

IT and business no longer exist in separate universes. IT is now a direct stakeholder in the creation of business value. The introduction of new IT-powered business-enablers in the enterprise ecosystem, like cloud computing, Big data, Enterprise Mobility, and Social Media, has made the Business–IT correlation more critical, even indispensable. Of course, tools like Enterprise Resource Planning (ERP) and Customer Relationship Management (CRM) continue to be part of the IT landscape, but it is these new enablers that have made Business and IT *integral* to each other. Quite clearly, IT has broken free of the back office, and it is time to redefine it using a new set of constituents.

Much of the technological revolution that we see around us is a result of diverse technologies *converging* to spawn new products and applications. The smartphone, laptop computer, IP-TV, and Voice-over-IP are some familiar examples of convergence from the IT and telecom world. It is common to use the term ICT (Information and Communication

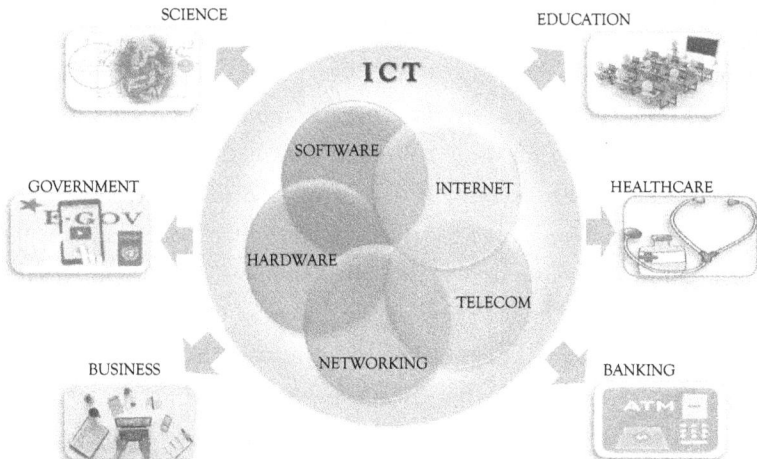

*Figure 3.1 ICT ecosystem*

Technology) to refer to *converged* IT, telecommunication, and media streams. ICT covers any product or service that can store, retrieve, manipulate, transmit, or receive information in digital form. While IT and telecom are primary *enablers* of ICT, the reach of ICT extends to every industry (Figure 3.1). Trends in ICT enable new developments—sometimes entirely new markets—in banking, health care, education, government, and other industry verticals.

Interestingly, there's an ICT development index (IDI), which is published by the International Telecommunication Union (ITU, A United Nations body). IDI measures and compares ICT performance of various countries on specific parameters based on ICT infrastructure, usage/adoption, and skills available. It's one of the most valuable tools for benchmarking the important indicators of information society globally. ICT is an indicator of the economic development of nations. Countries with higher ICT development index are in a higher per-capita income bracket, with better quality of life. With the decline in global poverty index, there has been increased ICT adoption.[4]

It would be beyond the scope of this book to go into all the social, political, economic, and environmental implications of ICT. Suffice it to say that ICT is the principal source of new opportunities to foster economic and social prosperity in developed as well as emerging economies.

The ITU report on Measuring the Information Society[4] supports our claim that all the major factors for technology-driven business growth are right in place, and the trends are positive. There was never a more opportune time to leverage the combined power of business and technology to create a positive impact across the economic spectrum.

The proliferation of the *Internet* and *mobile* networks is among the most visible consequences of ICT growth. The innovative use of the Internet and mobile technologies as the building blocks of enterprise-centric business solutions is driving the digital economy. This also stresses the need for stronger alignment between Business and IT.

In the remainder of this chapter, let us discuss some of the new technology trends spawned by the growth in Internet and mobile adoption that are making waves in today's business world, and how they are helping to shape the future of business.

The discourse that follows is meant for non-technologists, which most of us are. The use of terms that would make sense only to experts is, therefore, avoided. If terms like *platform, framework, virtualized, abstracted,* and *protocol* do not resonate with you, you are not alone. More importantly, you are in no danger. We have, therefore, avoided these terms here. The digital age has replaced the confusing jargon with new and more relatable concepts, which would be universally understood. Terms like cloud computing and social media, for example, are everyday terms that the average person relates with.

## Cloud Computing

Cloud refers to a *remote* cluster of *computing resources* (servers, storage, applications, and data) accessed by the user over a secure network or the Internet, as a logical extension of the user's device. In short, it is the place from where experiences are delivered on-demand via the Internet. The practice of using the cloud, rather than the local device, to store, manage, and process data is called cloud computing. Thus, if your data and applications are on a cloud, you can access them from *any* device. This allows us to view computing through an entirely new lens, with profound implications on the way information is accessed, retrieved, processed, managed, and stored.

Cloud-based computing resources are typically hosted by a cloud service provider (CSP) and made available to the user *on-demand.* The user may be charged by the CSP based on usage, quite along the lines of utility services like electricity and water. This is a paradigm shift from the earlier practice where you *owned* computing resources, and these were dedicated for your use alone. Cloud computing can be a very efficient way of utilizing computing power. One of the reasons cloud computing has gained traction with enterprises is the freedom it allows from having to procure capital equipment and the associated infrastructure (like real estate, power, and cooling), and instead leasing the computing resources *as a service.* Thus, cloud computing allows you to get what you require without the concomitant worries of support, obsolescence, depreciation, and capacity planning. There are some concerns over privacy and security as most companies are yet to come to terms with the idea of

*Figure 3.2  The Cloud*

keeping their critical data on a third party's server. These concerns are being addressed through new security approaches, but caution about the privacy of data is always a good thing. In my view, the cloud is no more or less secure than a private data-center, though the types of security concerns are different here (Figure 3.2).

A cloud can be Private, Public, or Hybrid (Figure 3.3). As the name suggests, a *private cloud* is exclusive to an enterprise. All resources within a private cloud operate with the sole purpose of providing a distinct and *secure* environment to a specific unit *only*. A private cloud can be the enterprise's own *data center*, which is an in-house facility with an organized set of servers, storage, and associated hardware and software components that collectively function as the "IT powerhouse" of the unit. Alternatively, this infrastructure could be hosted by a remote third-party *Infrastructure-as-a-Service (IaaS)* provider who takes care of the management and routine operational overheads on behalf of the client for a fee. In either event, a private cloud is a *single-tenancy* cloud computing environment. By contrast, a *public cloud* is a *multi*-tenancy cloud computing environment, where each client shares the computing resources with several other clients over the Internet. Many of the personal cloud-based

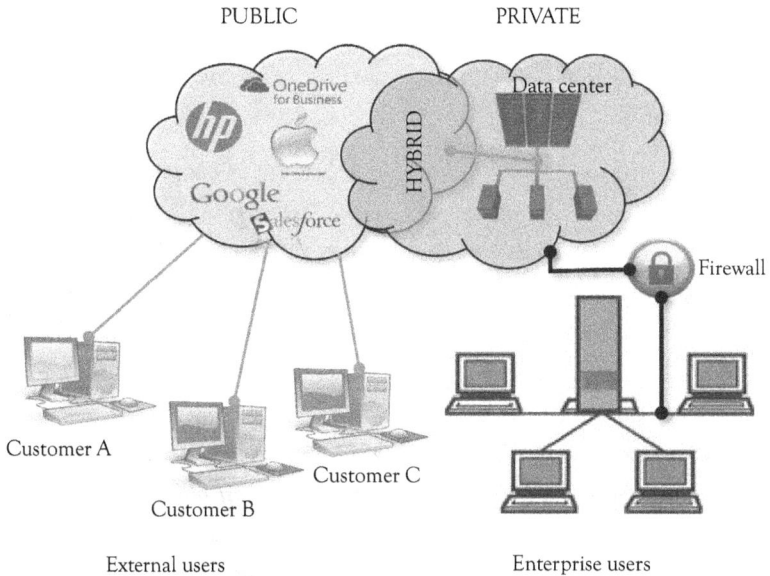

*Figure 3.3 Hybrid cloud*

services (like iCloud, OneDrive) that we use are examples of the public cloud. Enterprises usually prefer the *hybrid* model. A *hybrid cloud* is a cloud computing environment which makes use of a *mix* of existing private cloud infrastructure and available public cloud services, such as Salesforce.com, with orchestration between the two cloud environments to render the best of both worlds.

Cloud computing plays another very vital, but often ignored, *strategic* role in promoting Business–IT alignment. This is best explained with a real-life example.

---

**Example 3.1**

*I once participated in a panel discussion with a rather dark theme: "The Death of the CIO"! As a Chief Information Officer (CIO) myself, it is a no-brainer that I chose to argue against this prophecy. The idea behind the theme was that with the advent of cloud computing, there would be nothing for the CIO (read internal IT function) to do, since all the servers, storage, applications, and data would be managed by a third-party in some unseen location. So, the reasoning went, the CIO and his flock*

---

*would become a redundant entity (hence dead metaphorically). It was a tricky spot because I am a strong proponent of the cloud but not of the CIO's death!*

*I argued that cloud would indeed free the CIO of some of the routine operational issues, but in its place, a more strategic role would evolve. Most CIOs today spend far more time in just keeping the show going than on collaborating with Business. Cloud is, therefore, a boon to the CIO who can now pair shoulders with the business to advise and drive strategic solutions that would be of far greater value to the business than the monitoring of IT servers. Second, migration to enterprise-class cloud is not a fork-lift operation. It is an opportunity to reevaluate, consolidate, and revamp your IT architecture to better suit business needs and save costs in the bargain. This requires elaborate and ongoing planning in consultation with Business. Third, the CIO has a better opportunity than before to qualify and prioritize new business requirements, filter and bundle them consultatively, and interwork with the cloud service provider to deliver on time, cost, and quality targets set by the Business. The whole cloud operation, which is run by a partner, must be systematically managed with high efficiency, throughput, and security which places demands of its own on the CIO.*

*To conclude, the cloud is perhaps a metamorphosis of the CIO but certainly not the death of the CIO. It is a redefinition of the CIO as a more strategic enabler of business success through better-aligned Business and IT priorities.*

Cloud computing requires very close Business and IT interplay. Many of the critical business applications that are used by the internal teams (like Salesforce.com), as well as customer-impacting applications like CRM, are now cloud-hosted. Hosting applications on the cloud and rendering them over the Internet to users on a subscription basis is a popular cloud service, known as *Software-as-a-Service*, or SaaS. A lot of medium-sized enterprises are now relying on SaaS, even for routine business services like e-mail.

A strong BITA in the cloud-enabled world can bring many differentiated offerings to customers quickly. In a company that I worked for, there was an imminent requirement of the business to launch a mobile payment service. The Business and IT teams worked together to identify and evaluate a cloud service provider for this. The CSP agreed to customize an instance (a version of the mobile payments application) as per my company's requirements, and we were ready to offer this to the market in four weeks. During this period, IT worked diligently on assuring the right interfaces with backend applications, while Business tested the main functionality iteratively in live scenarios and performed quality audits. As we go forward, such interworking will become the norm to bring cloud-based services quickly to customers and take the lead in the market. This can only happen with strong and sustained Business–IT alignment.

## Big Data

Big data is another new idea that is very relevant to the times and hence making rapid strides into our business world. Big data means precisely that—when *data* becomes very *big* in its *volume* (size), *variety* (types), and *velocity* (throughput and speed of processing), it becomes, quite predictably, *Big data*. The fourth property generally associated with Big data is *veracity* (certainty and precision). True to this, we define Big data in terms of these four Vs. At the root of Big data is the abundance of data in the digital world, necessitating new methods for extraction of *value* from data.

The rate at which data is being created and transmitted today is well beyond our capacity to comprehend. There is an exponential growth in social, enterprise, and machine-generated data in the last five years and the rate of growth is expected to only increase from here. It is not just the volume of data that is staggering, but also the variety—from text messages to high-definition video. A lot of information on individual preferences, behaviors, and trends can be gleaned from this stream, but the question is, *how to do it* given the high volumes, staggering speeds, and wide variety? This is where Big data comes in.

The Vs that we referred to earlier are very briefly defined in Figure 3.4. The best way to understand them would perhaps be to consider the *changes* in these Vs in our lifetimes:

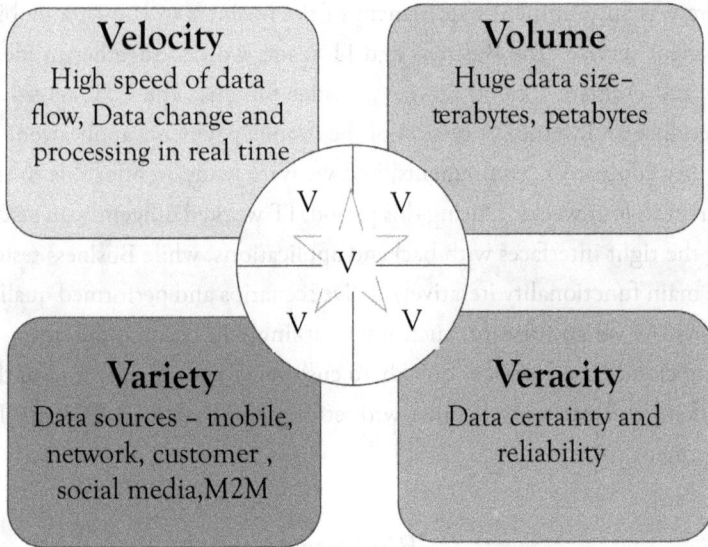

| Velocity | Volume |
|---|---|
| High speed of data flow, Data change and processing in real time | Huge data size— terabytes, petabytes |
| Variety | Veracity |
| Data sources – mobile, network, customer , social media,M2M | Data certainty and reliability |

*Figure 3.4  Big data—the 5 Vs*

**A. Velocity**—Batch → Periodic → Near-Real-time → Real-time → Data *Hose* (e.g., incessant Twitter feeds in a wide survey)

**B. Volume**—MB → GB → TB → PB → EB

**C. Variety**—Table → Database → Web, Photos, audio → Video, Unstructured → Social → Mobile → Mix of these

The V in the center of the diagram here represents *value*, to unleash which we require special techniques that can handle huge volumes, high velocity, and large variety, simultaneously. Big data has spawned many emerging technologies, most notably Machine Learning and Artificial intelligence, which use smart algorithms to extract value from Big data, leading to contextual responses (e.g., facial recognition).

In the enterprise context, data is meaningless if it does not lend itself to analysis, transform into useful information, and generate meaningful insights that support business decision making. While we are creating tons of data, do we have the tools and the skills to *process* (i.e., read, decipher, and classify) such huge volumes of data in reasonable timeframes? A business can no longer wait for days to get a response to a query on, say, a customer's proclivity to churn. The way Big data is processed is different from traditional data processing. Techniques are available that allow us to *fragment* the data across multiple nodes for *parallel* processing, resulting in a much faster response. Let me explain this with a simple example that surprisingly predates Big data by over a decade, but beautifully captures the essence of how we process Big data today.

*In 1999, the University of California at Berkeley conceived of a project that was nicknamed SETI@home.[5] SETI stands for Search for Extraterrestrial Intelligence and is an initiative focused on scanning the cosmos for signs of intelligent life. To search for intelligent signals in the vastness of deep space required several giant telescopes that could scan the skies, detect even very weak radio emissions with remarkable sensitivity, and send them to a centralized computer, which could record all of them and analyze them. Hopefully, somewhere amid all the radio noise, there was a signal sent by intelligent beings light years away! Unfortunately, finding this needle of a signal in the enormous haystack of data required almost unlimited processing time (and power) even on the largest and fastest computers in existence. The folks at the UCB stuck upon a rather bold but brilliant idea to solve this problem: Why not turn to a massively underutilized computing resource: the millions of personal computers (like your laptop) sitting on desks the world over, spending much of their time running mindless screensavers. Anyone with a PC could enlist as a participant in SETI@home, and the process was completely unobtrusive. This combined computing power was harnessed to process the mountain of SETI data, thus solving much of SETI's computing problem at a stroke. That is, they embarked upon the idea of fragmenting the vast received data and assigning it to multiple nodes (the vast number of PCs the world over), processing it in parallel, and finally feeding the processed data back to the centralized computer over the Internet. Brilliant indeed!*

This is also how Big data is processed. That is, the largest blocks of data are fragmented into smaller chunks, processed in parallel across multiple nodes (as PCs in the SETI example), and collated. This cuts down the total processing time from weeks to hours! I have run Big data projects and seen this for myself. At first, it almost seems like a miracle.

A fundamental limitation of Big data is its inability to lend itself to relational databases and desktop statistics. Given its size, structure, and speed, generation of meaningful information from Big data requires *advanced analytics* techniques. Therefore, it is not Big data alone, but its intersection with Advanced Analytics that can give a fresh insight into a completely new worldview. When you cross this intersection, you enter the world of *Big data analytics.*

Analytics is the process of deriving information from data. This information can be presented in the form of dashboards, tables, or text depending on the requirements of the end-user. This, in turn, can lead to useful insights that support business decision making. The world of Big data analytics is, however, quite different from our known and familiar world of desktop analytics (Figure 3.5). Traditional algorithms for processing information require the information to be in main memory, accessed through a *single* central processing unit (CPU). In Big data analytics, the sheer size and diversity of data do not allow it all to be in memory at the

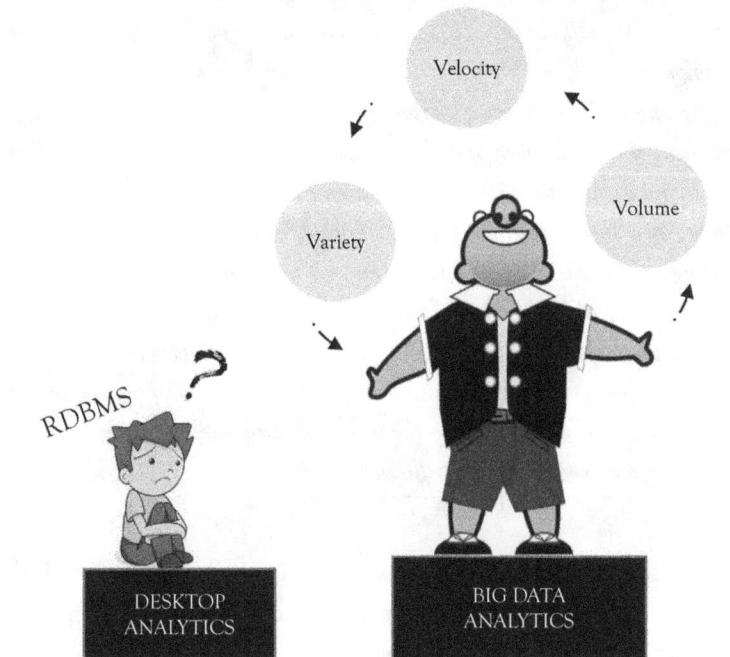

*Figure 3.5  Big data analytics*

same time in a single system, and hence it calls for *distributed processing* across a host of systems. The entire process of extracting value from data is a specialized discipline, which has given rise to a new branch of study called *data science* and whose proponents are called, as you guessed, data scientists, a much-coveted discipline today.

Big data is fast becoming a primary lever for gaining a competitive edge in a world that is increasingly dominated by data. It has become very relevant for marketing campaigns to leverage insights uncovered by Big data, which can then effectively personalize communication to individual customers of the brand. In addition to analyzing all the transactional data generated by businesses, it is important for companies to assimilate all the relevant information shared on *social media sites*, to provide solutions that are tailored to fit individual needs.

If brands want to reach a specific audience, they need to carefully analyze the adoption, usage, payment, and service satisfaction trends of consumers of the brand. This trend and behavior analysis of various customer segments is one of the leading pull factors for the enterprise adoption of Big data analytics as the gateway to smarter marketing campaigns and better management of customer experience.

For successful adoption of Big data, cooperation between leadership teams across Business and IT is crucial. The focus of CIOs today is on identifying opportunities to streamline business processes. The CIO must recognize the importance of managing customer expectations at each stage of the lifecycle, which, in turn, must spur the deployment of data management tools and processes to garner deeper customer insights. Ensuring requisite skill-set in the organization to derive gains from Big data is another critical battle that CIOs need to win.

With the advent of Big data technology, data has become an undisputed business asset as it is now possible to dive wide and deep into the ocean of data and generate useful business insights. Coupled with this is the fact that Big data is emerging concurrently with a host of complementary trends such as cloud computing, social media, enterprise mobility, and in-memory computing. We may see a very new kind of convergence which brings these trends together, to create THE enterprise architecture of the future. When this happens, the need for perfect alignment between Business and IT will be further accentuated. Enterprises on a strong BITA track *today* would thus be at a distinct competitive advantage.

## Enterprise Mobility

Somewhat contrary to popular thinking, mobility is not about *movement*. It is about *freedom*. Freedom has a direct impact on an individual's agility, which makes mobility both liberating and transformational. It is no surprise, therefore, that mobility is making rapid advances into every arena of human endeavor.

In the enterprise context as well, mobility means *freedom* from devices, platforms, networks, and of course, geography. Simply put, it means that access to what I hold important (e.g., a Document) is not restricted by the device I am holding in my hand, or by the network I am connected to (e.g., office LAN or public Wi-Fi or cellular network ) and certainly not by which part of the globe I happen to be in!

A lot of times, people equate mobility to Bring Your Own Device (BYOD). BYOD enables you to have seamless access to office and personal data without having to switch devices. True, this is mobility but only *one* of its many use cases. While some organizations disallow BYOD as their security concerns override the anticipated benefits, many are still taking a cautious approach to it, and typically allow e-mail and some employee apps (like leave, travel) only. There are, however, several smarter organizations that have built robust authentication and access control systems to embrace mobility in a much bigger way and reaped considerable benefits in productivity and employee morale.

The proliferation of mobile devices like smartphones and tablets has been a catalyst for mobility. Availability of abundant bandwidth has been another boost. However, the biggest driver for mobility has been the *hunger* for information anywhere and anytime. With the underlying device and network infrastructure in place, it was only a matter of time before smart business applications arrived on the scene to leverage mobility for business benefit.

**Example 3.2**

*A communications company in India leveraged a vast countrywide network of distributors and dealers for providing cellular connections to the populace. Traditionally, the company's territory sales manager (TSM) responsible for a patch routinely visited various distributors and dealers gathering information on sales, channel performance, forecasts, and so on, while assisting them in promotions. The data collected by the TSM was fed into a web-based application back in the main office as and when the TSM could visit, which was not very often given the requirement to be on the street, and the remoteness of some territories from the nearest office. The calculation of sales commissions across the hierarchy of distributors, dealers, sub-dealers (who could even be a grocery shop owner or the village milkman!) were frequently delayed for this reason. It was also not possible to track sales or achievements against sales targets on a regular basis. Management was unable to review territory-wise sales and plan timely interventions. They finally took to mobility as the solution. Each TSM was provided with a tablet that ran the mobile instance of the web-enabled application (earlier available in the office only) so that he could input data on the spot (or from the nearest network zone), and thus track and report sales by distributor, dealer, and sub-dealer. This application instantly presented the territory sales performance to the TSM. It enabled all data to be captured in near real-time and allowed channel commissions and sales information to be available on request. The back-end system could collate the performance of all TSMs in a zone and feed the results to the zonal sales manager, and so on up to the level of regional Chief Operating Officer (COO). The COO now had a report on the previous day's sales in his mailbox at 9:00 a.m. each morning, which earlier used to be an end-of-month activity. This is a clear instance where a mobility solution not only boosted internal efficiency but also increased the scope for higher penetration into the market, and trade satisfaction (faster commissions). It also allowed the sales managers to do lightweight operations, like travel expense reporting, while on the move using the tablet, avoiding the need to check in at the office. Most importantly, it gave an insight into where he stood with respect to achievements against sales targets at any instant!*

Mobility is perhaps the single biggest game changer in the enterprise world today. As we said, mobility is enabled by a dynamic device ecosystem, an abundance of bandwidth, and an array of applications seamlessly coming together to satisfy a growing hunger for information anytime and anywhere. It has changed behaviors across the organization and brought in a new culture—be it the average employee using BYOD, or the territory sales manager with his mobile enabled device and application, or even the company CEO, as the next example shows.

---

**Example 3.3**

*The CEO of a well-known Indian software services company was on a visit to Japan, where he was to meet one of his most important clients. This meeting was to be with six members of the senior staff of the client company, including their MD. The importance of their time and the need to be up-to-date to make the best use of the 30 minutes allotted for the meeting was not lost on the visiting CEO. While he was on the 45-minute car ride from his earlier meeting to this one, he used a mobile enterprise app to get a complete dossier on his tablet PC, giving the profiles, with photographs, of each client delegate and who from this CEO's organization met him/her last and when. Some data priming, of course, had already been done by the local office for their CEO's visit! Next, a quick status of the key projects, billing information, major complaints, and resolution state as of that morning was populated through the app on his tablet. Thus, when the CEO arrived for the meeting, he knew everyone by face, name, function, preferences, and grievances. I imagine the meeting went quite well, as everyone, and not least the Japanese, appreciate a good preparation and astute management of time.*

---

Mobile solutions (like in the examples above) offer better communications, faster and more accurate decision making, and better customer service, all of which lead to a competitive advantage for the business. For example, an employee at the client site may be able to access any required information on the company's products and solutions from the cloud storage through his device (laptop, tablet, even smartphone) to show what his customer *needs*, as he is no longer confined to stuff that is on his laptop! He may also connect remote experts through online chat or video to resolve customer complaints while on the site.

## What makes enterprise mobility possible

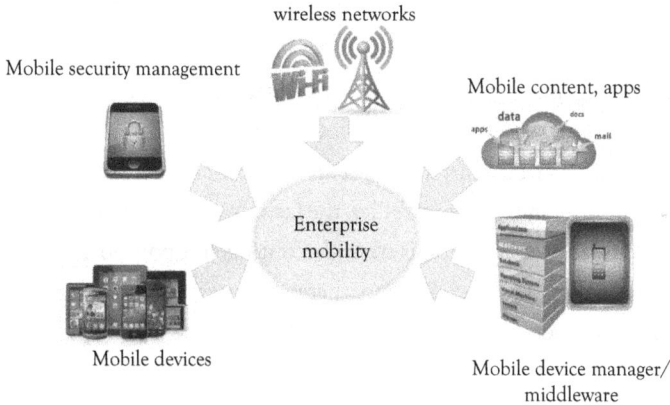

*Figure 3.6 Enterprise mobility*

Enterprise mobility (Figure 3.6) is an intelligent offshoot of the existing mobility ecosystem. You can offer rudimentary (i.e., with *limited* ability to manage and control what you are rendering) services leveraging the existing wireless network infrastructure, a server somewhere that hosts data, a few mobile applications, and all the available smart handheld devices with the employees. To give it a tinge of robustness, however, you need mobile security management and authentication system for preventing misuse and unauthorized access. To offer these enhanced services to the user base, a Mobile Device Manager (MDM) is required. The MDM is a client–server system, which enables end-users to benefit from plug-and-play data services. The MDM server is a centralized component, hosted by the service provider, which sends out various management commands to the mobile device. The MDM *client* here is a piece of software running on the end-device itself. How many times have you had to call the service provider's desk to configure a new device you have acquired? All that the service rep does is to send you a link and ask you to *activate* it from your device. This essentially installs (downloads) the client on your device, and the MDM takes over from there, insulating you from complex configuration procedures. Some versions of MDM server also take care of accounting and authentication of the user.

One of the biggest benefits of mobility is the level of engagement it enables with the customer. The availability of information wherever and whenever you want does give you an edge that is hard to beat. Ability to provide better customer service remains a primary driver for adoption of mobility by enterprises.

The enterprise world today seeks increased sales and better customer service, lower expenses, improved productivity, and happier employees. It so happens that mobility provides *all* of these benefits and more. The earlier you adopt enterprise mobility, the faster you can achieve these benefits. Of course, this adoption is strongly contingent upon close step-locking between Business and IT, and therefore, organizations with strong BITA have a much higher chance of benefitting from mobility.

## Social Media

Most of us today are part of some social media network. Social media (SM) has crossed all boundaries of age, race, status, income, and nationality. It has made the world a smaller, better informed, and more connected place. SM, being a vital element of the redefined enterprise ecosystem, is another constituent that depends on a strong BITA to leverage its potential as a driver of business growth.

SM collectively refers to tools, channels, and applications that allow the creation, sharing, and exchange of content—like messages, information, pictures/video, and files—between people over the Internet. More pertinently, SM is a collective term for media that promote online collaboration among communities. Social media is a result of preexisting technology building blocks, like IP-centric networks, webservers, cloud, devices, and applications coming together to fulfill an inherent human need to mix and mingle.

Social media is just about everywhere. Websites and applications dedicated to a wide range of collaborative activities are among the many types of social media that surround us. While all these cannot be listed here, the table in Figure 3.7 depicts some of the more prevalent ones.

| Type of SM | Some Examples of Applications and Websites |
|---|---|
| Social networking | hi5 facebook *TAGGED* myspace orkut bebo |
| Business networking | Linked in plaxo XING |
| Discussion boards, forums | Google DIS boards.com grouply Big Boards |
| Social streams | twitter echo status.net |
| Messaging and chat | WhatsApp Skype Viber |
| Pictures and video | You Tube Picasa flickr •• Dailymotion |
| Music | Rhapsody PANDORA |
| Wiki | WIKIPEDIA wikispaces TWiki |
| Q & A | Answers.com YAHOO! Answers AllExperts |
| Comments | DISQUS intensedebate |
| Collaboration | threadbox Office Live |
| Blogging | Blogger tumblr. TypePad |
| Social commerce | Milo Bazaarvoice GROUPON |
| Enterprise | tibbr yammer salesforce Lync Skype |
| Crowd wisdom | BuzzFeed Storify |
| Location | highlight DOPPLR |

*Figure 3.7 A sample of the social media universe*

Again, this is not the entire social media universe, neither in terms of types of SM nor applications and websites against each type. Further, let's not forget that it is an expanding universe.

**Example 3.4**

*As CIO, one of my aspirations was to connect, at least every quarter, with the IT users (read all employees, partners) across the organization, dispersed across 70+ offices in the country. For most people, IT, like oxygen, is noticed only by its absence—you feel choked when it is not there but take it for granted while it is! I felt that there was a strong need for open, interactive sessions with all users to deliver an update on new developments in technology, listen to and address user grievances, get a firsthand feel of how things were shaping up on the market front, and take suggestions on how IT could better support the business in the field. The problem was how to simultaneously and interactively cover all employees without going into the elaborate arrangement of video cameras, High-definition (HD) TVs, microphones, speakers, tons of bandwidth, assembly halls, and so on. I also did not want employees to take time away from their work for these*

> *sessions. As a solution, the CIO-Online virtual chat room was created—a product of social media. The CIO-Online session projected my audio and visual on all participating employees' laptops, who could see and hear me, as well as type in their questions and viewpoints for me in the message box. Users could also speak their views with permission (token), in which case their audio and visual could pop-up on everyone's screen. The token avoided multiple people speaking at once. After the question, I would retrieve control and provide my response for everyone's benefit. We used a popular version of an enterprise messaging platform, a client of which was embedded in every laptop provided by the company. Thus, we could have a secure interactive session, give the users—particularly the remote ones— direct contact with management, achieve two-way learning, and ensure that any pending grievances were addressed. All this at virtually no cost, achieved without anyone having to leave their workstations! The sessions were immensely popular and went a long way in boosting collaboration between IT and users.*

Since SM allows instant communication with many constituents, it is an excellent tool for campaigns and promotions by companies. Many enterprises are talking to their customers on Facebook, Twitter, and other social platforms, both on a collective and individual level. However, a lot more creative instance of SM usage is the *reverse* communication channel. That is, *consumers* sharing information on the product or service with the vendor, or among themselves. By using special programs like web crawlers, companies can get crucial data, which offers insights into the sentiments expressed by customers on social media, analyze these, and use the results to make timely course corrections. In fact, *sentiments analytics* is emerging as a field on its own, given its relevance to companies and consumers alike. It was once said that the voice of one disgruntled customer could reach 10 others. Social media just made it a million others! It is not hard to imagine the profound impact of this on companies' reputations and revenues.

Given the rising impact of social media on business, many enterprises have implemented distinct *social media strategies*. A few examples: DELL used SM as a channel for generating sales, perhaps one of the first examples of leveraging the power of social media. Comcast used SM to reach out to customers in need of support. Starbucks used social media to give a voice to their customers to propagate new product ideas. All these (and other) examples ride on the unprecedented reach enabled by SM and the opportunity provided by SM for businesses to interactively embrace their customers at last.

Using SM as part of business strategy makes sound sense given the payback. The two-way engagement path enables you to *measure* the reach, influence, traffic, and transactions relating to your market audience. This, in turn, allows you to analyze the results for timely insights into preferences, sentiments, views, and ideas relating to your offerings. SM underlines the need for strong integration between Business and IT to derive these insights and use them for enhancing sales and customer experience.

## Customer Experience Management

Like social media, customer experience management (CEM) is not a technological evolution by itself. It is a system that uses some of the building blocks of modern technology to fulfill the primary business need to engage, and stay engaged, with customers.

The core premise of CEM is that customers do not buy technology. They buy experiences. Thus, CEM is focused on the management of the complete *lifecycle* of the customer. The customer's view about a provider is influenced by various touchpoints that the customer comes across—from the pre-purchasing stage to post-sales support—and CEM views each of these touch points as an opportunity to improve the customer's experience and build loyalty and advocacy—the ultimate goals of CEM.

The pictorial representation shown in Figure 3.8 is a construction of the CEM workflow across all touch points.

In a nutshell, the figure highlights how CEM makes use of IT tools and infrastructure to convert customer *data* into meaningful *insights* that can be leveraged to create an effective customer strategy, which is then embedded into the various touch points across the lifecycle. The process is cyclic, enabling *continuous improvement*, which is quite useful, as customer expectations are always progressive and keep going up a few notches with every positive experience!

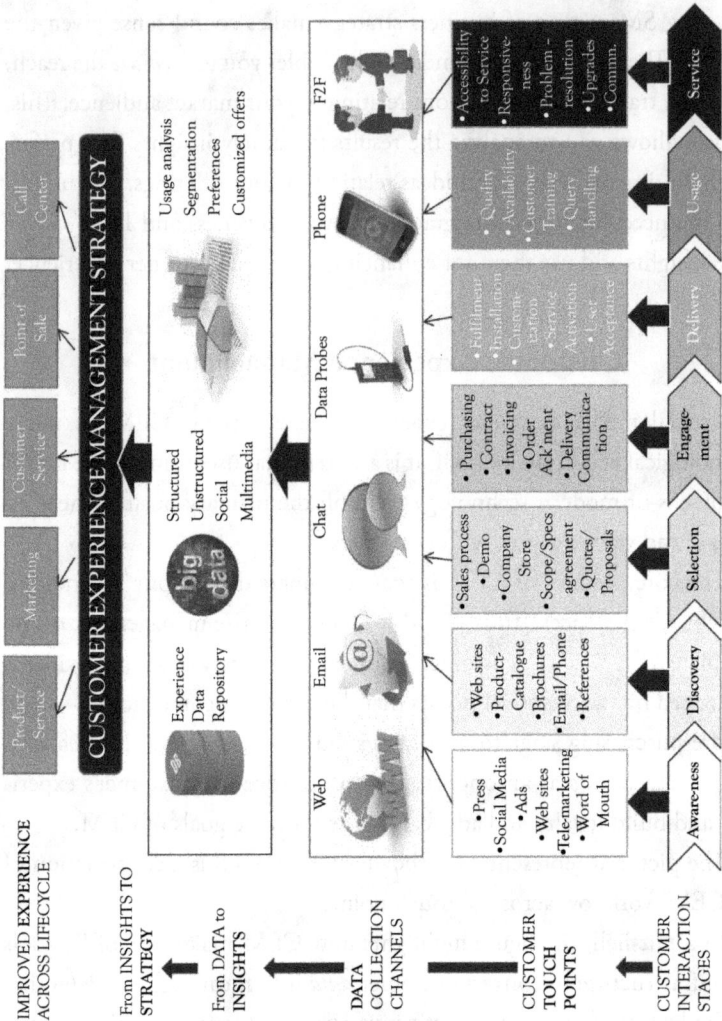

*Figure 3.8 Customer experience management*

---

**Example 3.5**

*One of the problems every telecom operator faces is customer churn, especially with the advent of mobile number portability (MNP). An operator typically gets both churning-in (which is good) and churning-out (which is bad) customers in a given month, and the strategy is obviously to increase the in-churners and minimize, if not eliminate, the out-churners. Before CEM, it was not possible to get accurate insights into the reasons for churn. One of the telecom operators in India was particularly perplexed about the churn situation. This company had launched a very compelling customer loyalty and retention program, driven down its call rates to one of the lowest in the market, and improved its customer service levels. But despite all this, it found the churn-out rate still increasing month on month. Curiously, it scored among the highest on the customer satisfaction scores! Then why should customers churn out? The company (let's call it X) adopted CEM to gain deeper insights into customer behavior to solve this mystery. What it discovered was quite insightful. India has a predominantly (95 percent) prepaid mobile subscriber base. A few years ago, the trend had picked up for many folks to keep two phones instead of one, or two SIMs in one phone. Due to lower on-net (i.e., within the same operator's network) calling rates, customers preferred their subscriptions (including family members') to be from the same operator. A substantial part of X's customers was in this segment. Of late, the price differential of on-net calling rates had diminished to the point of irrelevance, while the need for uninterrupted data connectivity was becoming paramount. Due to this, customers did not see any benefit of two subscriptions from the same operator. It was more compelling for customers to move one SIM to a different operator to safeguard against service interruptions. This led to the higher churn for X. It was indeed an elusive root cause, something that was only stumbled upon through deep probing enabled by CEM. As of writing this story, X is still working on an effective strategy to counter the situation. But knowing the root cause is half the battle won!*

---

There are many examples that demonstrate the relevance of CEM in aligning more closely to customer expectations at different stages of the life cycle, from across industries. A leading bank in India had many customers complaining that the initial passcode provided by the bank with new debit cards was declared invalid by ATMs. It emerged that the validity of the passcode was five days from dispatch, and on average, three were consumed in the parcel delivery. For many customers, who visited the ATM two or more days later, the code was void even before they started! Such insights are far more easily possible with CEM than through traditional means.

For driving customer loyalty, operational efficiency, and new revenue streams in an environment characterized by evolving technology, changing expectations, and hypercompetition, customer experience management plays a pivotal role. Customers are justifiably demanding more of their service providers today and managing customer experience as a discipline goes a long way in improving every interaction through the lifecycle. Most customer-focused organizations achieve this through the deployment of tools and processes to garner deeper customer insights. But more importantly, this environment requires a responsive customer service organization and a dynamic information technology ecosystem working seamlessly together to implement the CEM strategy.

CEM is focused on understanding customers' preferences and expectations based on their behavior *through the lifecycle* and using these to calibrate the customer service strategy. Its focus extends much beyond problem resolution or incident management.

Big data is expected to play an increasingly important role in the institutionalization of CEM. Big data enables us to reach the bottom of the pyramid and target the right group of customers for, say, a new campaign or service. Today the focus of every service organization is on customer loyalty and retention. And retaining a customer requires you to be able to differentiate your offering from the rest. Which, in turn, means providing an individualized and special experience to each customer tailored to his or her preferences. A strong alignment between Business and IT is thus at the core of CEM and organizations with a stronger BITA have a clear edge in attaining a loyal customer base, indisputably the biggest asset for any business.

In this chapter, we have introduced some of the new technological developments that are already well-entrenched in modern business and are expected to play an increasingly dominant role in the business of the future. These are the building blocks using which the technology-driven business edifices of the future will be constructed. As this happens, technology will play an enhanced role in driving business success, creating an environment in which technology and business will be inseparable from each other. Figure 3.9 depicts the gradual convergence of Business and Technology over the ages until they *fuse* in the digital age.

There are, of course, many other trends emerging, or have already emerged, which we have not touched upon here. These include the Internet of Things, Artificial Intelligence, Machine Learning, Merged Reality, and Blockchain on one level, and advanced encryption and data privacy, packaged applications, mass outreach programs (like education, health, governance, location-based services, etc.) on another, all driven by the intersection of existing technologies with each other and with business.

The sun will soon set on some of the established systems, especially the proprietary or bespoke ones. Stand-alone (not interoperable or networkable) and special-purpose devices among others do not appear to have a bright future. Hardware will be increasingly commoditized with software bringing in the needed differentiation. *Consumption* devices like smartphones, tablets, book readers will be distinct from and more prolific than *creation* devices like laptops, stand-alone cameras, and 3-Dimensional (3-D) printers.

Telecom companies, being key players in the ICT game, will no longer be content with being providers of dumb *pipes* (a euphemism for communication channel). They will migrate from being connectivity providers

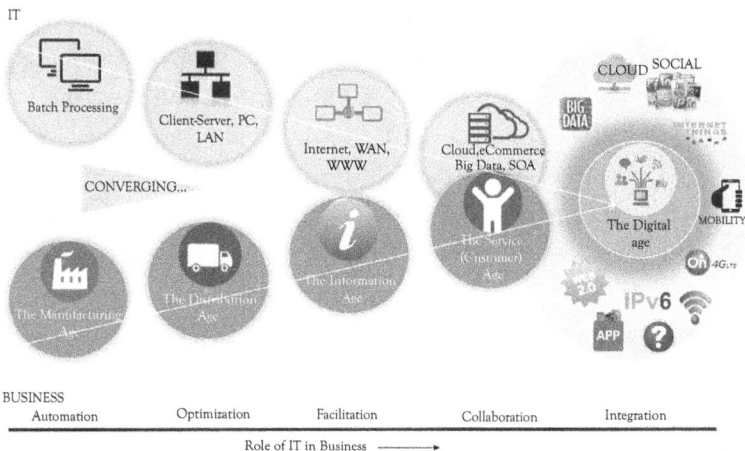

*Figure 3.9 Convergence of business and technology*

to *service* providers. Thus, there will be an increased collaboration with the so-called over-the-top invaders to create a more seamless ecosystem and smarter telecom networks. The performance of optical communication networks will continue to grow by a factor of 8 to 10 times every three years, making bandwidth more abundant. On the wireless side, new generations of technology—both cellular and Wi-Fi—will continue to evolve. While they may not catch up with optical networks in the bandwidth department, they will more than makeup for this by enabling even more seamless mobility.

On the IT software side, we can expect a higher prevalence of *object-oriented* technology (like Java), which enables the development of self-contained units of software that can be shared. Nonstandard software interfaces, architectures, and applications will be set aside, as standardization will become the norm since it ensures portability.

On the infrastructure segment, alongside increasing dominance of cloud computing, particularly SaaS and IaaS, we should witness the phasing out of dedicated machines and the new architectures will be increasingly based on *virtual* machines, which are emulations of (real) servers for hosting applications dynamically. This virtualization will lead to far more efficient utilization of IT resources.

With the sun rising on a host of new technologies while setting on others, it is clear that the future is going to be more different from the present than the present is from the past. The boundaries of technological growth will be drawn only by human imagination.

IT has come a long way from centralized mainframes, batch-processing minicomputers, and Y2K. So has Business. Established systems have been demolished to pave the way for a new order. Figure 3.9 depicts the journey of Business and IT through the ages to a final state of full convergence, heralding the dawn of the *digital age*. Here, your speed determines your survival. If trends are anything to go by, the advent of each transformative technology will emphasize the need for *stronger* BITA. The core principles of BITA, which we discussed in Chapter 2, will, however, continue to hold in the altered Business–IT landscape. Companies and individuals who are strong on BITA through its early infusion in their belief systems will have far higher growth—and survival—prospects in the digital economy, which is what we shall discuss next.

# CHAPTER 4

# The Digital Economy and What BITA Has To Do with It

Businesses traditionally define themselves by their *core competence*, with technology being at best an enabler. For example, a progressive retail business may view itself as a *merchandising* company that uses technology. Let's shift our perspective for a minute. Can this business be viewed as a *technology* company that does merchandising? If the answer is yes, this business is almost certainly a part of an emerging new world order. In fact, much before the advent of this new order, the above viewpoint was aptly stated by UPS: "We used to be a trucking company that used technology. We are now a technology company that uses trucks." Now think about *your* business in these terms.

Digital technology has permeated the creation, distribution, trade, and consumption of countless products and services across the globe. In other words, *the ecosystem of digital computing and communication technologies* has engulfed economic activity, giving rise to what has come to be known as the digital economy. While technologies like cloud, Big data, mobility, and social media are essential components, it is their widespread application, particularly in business, that has resulted in the thriving ecosystem that forms the digital economy.

We browsed the history of information technology in Chapter 1. If we take a quick peek into the history of *business,* we see that early economic activity was driven primarily by the twin engines of *production* and *distribution* of goods, and hence was bounded by raw material (natural resources), labor, and capital.[6] The value of intellectual property and by extension, technological innovation, was ignored entirely.

When digital technology first made an appearance, it was only in isolated pockets, limited by the *digital divide*—an *inequality* regarding access and use of information and communication technologies (ICT). For a business to thrive in the digital economy, the first condition was the abolishment of the digital divide. While its complete elimination is a rather lofty goal and something the world cannot wait for, the twin revolutions spawned by the Internet and mobile technology have considerably narrowed the digital divide, creating the right conditions for the digital economy to thrive.

Incidentally, the digital economy is not just about trade and commerce. It's a *way of life* in which digital technology blends seamlessly with almost every sphere of human activity. Let's look at a few familiar examples.

**Photography:** Until about the advent of the new millennium, photography was quite different from what it is today. Not everyone had a camera. Those who did were not always carrying it with them. Taking a picture was thus rarely impromptu. It was a process extending for days or weeks, from buying a reel of film, to getting the photos developed and printed. How different from just pulling out your mobile phone and clicking a picture, then sharing it next instant over social media with virtually anyone in the world—all in a matter of seconds.

**Banking:** Remember the days when every time you needed a bit of cash, you had to go up to the bank (within the working hours), queue up in front of the (human) teller, submit a requisition, and get the cash handed to you over the counter through a small window in the glass? Banking was never fun and very seldom quick. Things have changed with ATMs and more recently with Internet and mobile banking as we know. This is enabled by having all relevant constituents of a banking system—customers, branches, ATMs—on a digital network, which is readily and conveniently accessible.

**Shopping:** Digital technology has profoundly changed our shopping ways. We walk into the shop as much better-informed customers having done the due research on product specs, variety, and pricing on the Internet. We are provided with a choice of payment options through networked payment machines that are linked to our bank. Our purchasing trends are analyzed in real time to inform us of special offers on products that may be of interest. Lastly, the depleted inventory level at the store is automatically updated to trigger next reordering so that stock-out situations are rare. If, however, we are still not sufficiently immersed in the digital experience, we always have the option of buying stuff online while never leaving the comfort of our sitting room.

**Transportation and Navigation:** When I was younger, venturing into a new territory almost always meant stopping passersby for directions. Route planning for long distance travel was a manual and often cumbersome exercise. For example, you could never be sure how much to stock up on fuel and supplies since there was no way of knowing the location of filling stations and restaurants on the road, even if you could figure out the route. Cutting to the present, we all have map software on our phones or tablets and are therefore rarely "in the woods." We also know traffic patterns and alternative routes to get to our destination in the quickest possible time. This is enabled through the blending of satellite imagery with mobile data network and intelligent application software.

There are many other examples from our day-to-day experiences that emphasize the role of digital technology in transforming our lives. Just reflect on the way we now call for taxis, pay our utility bills, or book tickets for movie shows, as compared to 10 years ago. Even governments have forayed into the digital space through various e-governance initiatives.

Let's turn our attention to the business dimension of the digital economy, which is epitomized by the *digital enterprise*, and see how the digital economy has expanded horizons *and* made the world a smaller place at the same time.

The digital enterprise is a product of the digital economy. It is a web-based enterprise surrounded by an ecosystem of technology (ICT), partners (ecosystem alliances), influencers (external environment), and markets (market/consumers), as in Figure 4.1. Successful digital enterprises draw from the enabling constituents of the ecosystem to assure their sustenance and growth.

There are many examples of medium and large enterprises going digital and transforming themselves in the process, leveraging the various constituents of the digital enterprise ecosystem. A few cases in point are Starbucks, Nespresso, McDonald's, Disney, T-Mobile, and Fujifilm, which the interested reader may like to study.[7] Another example, which may resonate with many in India, is presented below.

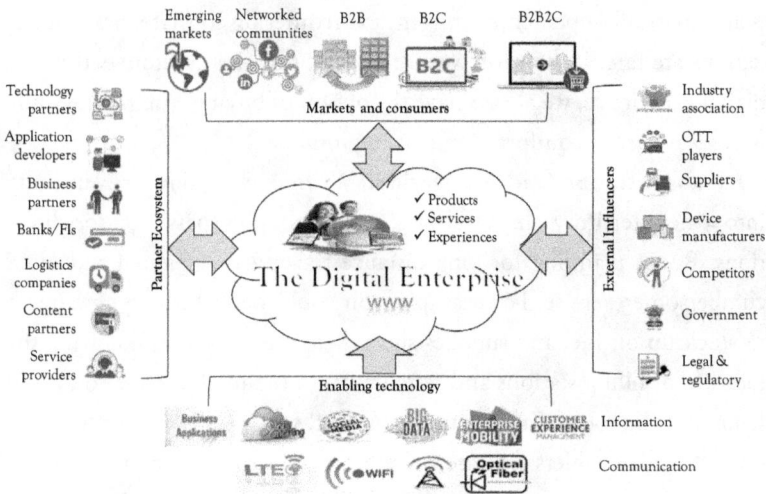

*Figure 4.1 Digital enterprise ecosystem*

---

**Example 4.1**

*Before the turn of the millennium, personal travel in India was mostly by train as it was very economical. However, this required reserving your seat or berth (if overnight journey) in advance. The process meant going to the city reservation office, filling up a form, queuing up before the ticket window for up to two hours, and finally presenting the form to a flustered clerk who almost always had an air of "take it or leave it" about him or her. At the end of it all, you may well be told that no seats or berths are available, so you may need to replan the travel and repeat the process! It wasn't fun.*

*Over time, the system changed from the above completely manual one to a more automated version, which enabled the same clerk to punch information into a computer terminal at his window. In time, this gave way to an online system that was linked over the Internet, and finally to a mobile-enabled system that lets passengers reserve their seats themselves from laptops or smartphones. Instead of a paper version, you can now travel with just an image of the ticket that is instantly delivered to your phone! The Internet based system, which has kept pace with technological developments, was originally conceived in 1999 by the Indian Railway Catering and Tourism Corporation*

*(IRCTC) and is called IRCTC.com. It is not only that you can make your bookings online from anywhere, any time, and using any device. The way the train options and availability information are presented makes it very convenient, even exciting, to plan and undertake train travel.*

*Before concluding that this is no different from other online travel portals, consider some facts about IRCRC.com:*

- *It handles well over a million ticket bookings on an average day.*
- *It is the biggest e-commerce service in India, more than double of the next one in volumes handled.*
- *The system deals with about 13,000 trains of different types; seven or eight classes of travel; various types of reservation/ ticket statuses; concessions (senior citizens, students, disabled, armed forces); seasonal changes at short notices; journey breaks and onward journeys, among others.*
- *IRCTC as a public body had to win against massive bureau- cracy, fund shortages, cultural bottlenecks, and a lack of political will at every step of the way.*

*Nowhere has the impact of technology on daily life been higher—in terms of where we were to where we are—than in the Indian Rail Reservation system. The technologies that have gone into building IRCTC.com include web technologies (Server/Client-side program- ming), security and authentication (encryption, fraud prevention), analytics, advertising platform, and payment gateways, among others.*

*The IRCTC system uses a strong technology foundation, which includes cloud, Big data, and mobility. It leverages a partner ecosystem of application (app) developers, advertisers, and others. It also meets the requirements of the external environment of government regula- tor, travel industry, air/international links, hotels, and so on. All this is geared toward delivering B2C (mostly) and B2B service to its vast customer base (market). It thus leverages all four pillars of the digital*

> *ecosystem that we introduced earlier and offers a great example of how technology can transform an enterprise, regardless of volume, traffic, and complexity considerations, to simplify life for the denizens of a digital world.*

In varying measures, all digital businesses follow this model, relying on the interplay with the ecosystem constituents within each of the four pillars.

As the spread of digital increases, you come across more and more *apps* becoming available. "App" has become a euphemism for a digital service. These apps sit on top of a layered stack, most of which is invisible to the end-user. When you invoke an app, you are inviting a whole *range* of disruptive forces to participate in your digital experience. The app is only the tip of the digital iceberg (Figure 4.2).

While the B2C and B2B models are more widespread, the digital economy also backs the C2C (consumer to consumer) model. Here, anyone can become a buyer and/or a seller. Many examples exist (like renting residential premises), some of which are quite inventive.

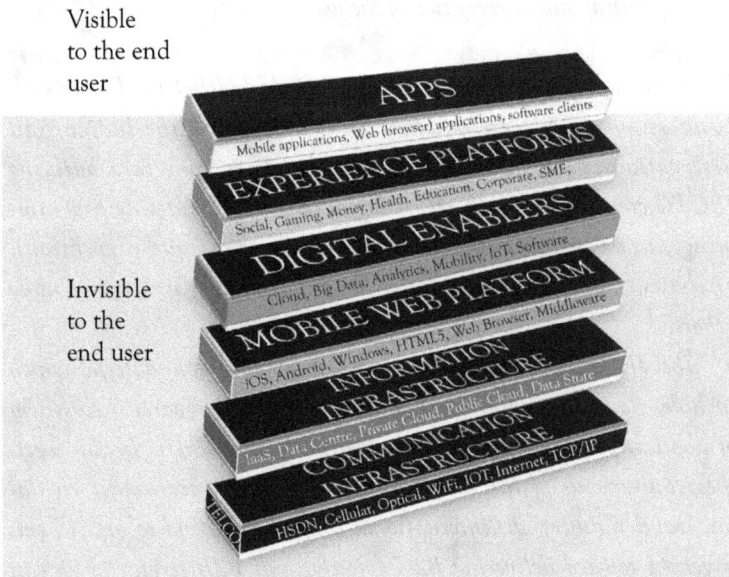

*Figure 4.2  The digital iceberg*

**Example 4.2**

*Just the other day, as my wife and I were busy packing for a road trip to Nainital (a hill-station about six hours' drive from Delhi), our nephew came in and suggested a mobile app which I could use to advertise my trip. This would enable, he said, another couple somewhere in Delhi who may be scouting for travel options to Nainital on the same day to connect with us and use the available capacity of our car for their journey. In the bargain, we would get paid enough to cover the cost of fuel and more! Plus, we could make good friends, he insisted! While our response was a No, Thank You! (this didn't quite fit in with our holiday plans), I found it quite amusing. The digital economy is sure opening new ways of making a business out of anything, such as the unoccupied seats in my car!*

**Example 4.3**

*Though not strictly C2C, another example of how the digital economy opens interesting avenues is evident in this business started by an enterprising lady in a suburb of Delhi. Utilizing her vacant apartment, she offers pest-free closet-storage for heavy dresses like gowns and tuxes, which are expensive but used seldom. For most apartment-dwellers in the city, these passive dresses disproportionately eat up their limited wardrobe space. This lady solves that problem for you through a mobile app at a nominal base rental and additional charges for optional services like pickup and delivery, laundering and so on, for which she has built partnerships with launderers, deliverers, and packagers. A "cloud-storage" of a different kind, some might say!*

Very few of us would doubt that if there is one thing quite certain about the future, it is digital dominance. Enterprises beating an early path to digital are therefore at a clear and unbeatable advantage.

The digital transformation of an enterprise is a well-thought-out process that typically originates in an idea (or vision) around the innovative use of digital technology and culminates in a clear competitive advantage to the business, as shown (Figure 4.3). Simply put, digital transformation is about boosting your business by leveraging new advances in digital

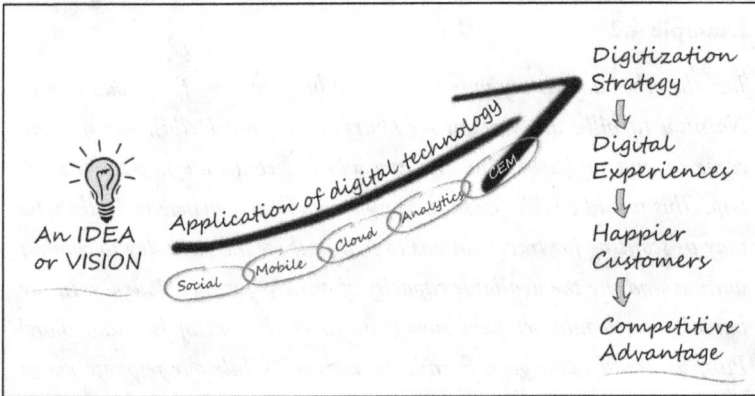

*Figure 4.3 The power of an idea in the digital world*

technology. It applies universally and certainly to *your* business. Think about how you could do this.

## Gearing Up to Go Digital

Digital transformation is not as daunting a venture as many think it to be. It is crucial, however, to not lose sight of some important signposts along the road:

- The biggest inhibitor to digital adoption in an organization is not the stage of its technological evolution but the mental unpreparedness of its people. Overcoming this may consume precious months or years during which your competition may get an unsurpassable lead. As a first step, therefore, make sure that *everyone* on the bus shares the digital vision, believes in it, and is passionate about its accomplishment. This always works top-down and must be reinforced by the leadership at every opportunity.
- For businesses and enterprises in the digital economy, *a strong Business–IT alignment (BITA) is the new normal.* The digital economy *demands* a strong BITA. Business has become so closely intertwined with Technology that lack of alignment between Business and Technology is the surest recipe for disaster. We shall see how your enterprise measures up on the BITA index in a subsequent chapter.

- Perhaps the biggest threat to traditional enterprises aiming to go digital is the lowering of entry barriers by the digital wave. New entrants often exhibit greater flexibility and can scale up much faster and at considerably lower costs. This stresses the need to be very nimble and fleet-footed. Time is not on your side if you are a large monolithic player striving to achieve, or retain, supremacy in the digital age. But innovation is.

- The digital economy is driven by continuous innovation in products, services, distribution channels, payment methods, and business models. It may not be possible, or feasible, for one company to have expertise in all these segments. The digital value chain may, therefore, have many participants, who may, in other circumstances, be competing. This *coopetition* is not an exception but a norm in the digital age, with a single offering carrying several integrated elements to deliver a comprehensive experience to the consumer.

- Digital transformation is not a destination but a journey. Each innovation may propagate a series of new possibilities, and the cycle repeats itself. Consequently, once you come up with a digital strategy and business model, and launch yourself as a digital enterprise, you cannot rest on your laurels. As a rule, never stop seeking fresh ideas and keeping your ears tuned to the customer's voice. More companies have failed due to complacency than owing to an unviable product idea or poorly designed business model.

There is, unfortunately, no time-tested standard flow that works for all enterprises seeking to embark on the digital journey. Like people, enterprises are unique and at different stages of (digital) evolution. Even so, companies on the digital transformation path follow some typical steps, which include the following:

### Establish a Sense of Urgency

The start of the digital journey is not something you put in your three-year business plan. The time is *now*. This sense of urgency is not required only in the CEO, CIO, or the company's digital champion. There must be a visible and palpable wave of excitement *sweeping the enterprise*, reinforced through constant motivational communication by the leadership.

### Create a Shared Mission and Vision for the Enterprise

A digital transformation is about journeying into the future. The leadership must ensure that *everyone* on this journey is clear and enthusiastic about its mission (what you must do) and vision (who you intend to become) through constant reinforcement and by "walking the talk." Freeloaders and skeptics have no place here. Further, to be shared and believed, your mission and vision must present a simple yet inspiring image of the future. Remember that technology is *not* the purpose for which the enterprise exists. It is only a means to achieve it. Hence your mission statement may *not* be "We exist to provide online access to cloud-based portfolio information over high-speed communication channels to maximize the earnings of our customers," but the rather more mundane yet purposeful: "We help our investors achieve the best returns on their portfolio in the quickest time."

### Prepare a Transformation Blueprint

Between the mission and the strategy is the critical phase of developing a blueprint, or a guide for executing the transformation project. This involves analysis and preparation for getting answers to relevant questions about the internal and external factors that can have an impact on the viability of the project. A few relevant questions would be:

- In what way will digital transformation impact our current business model?
- How does it affect our positioning in the value chain?
- How will it help us identify and enter new business areas?
- How vulnerable will we be to disruptions from new entrants?
- Which new capabilities are needed to become an industry leader?

## Define Your Digital Transformation Strategy

A strategy is nothing but a plan to achieve your mission (what and how?). While defining the digital strategy for your enterprise, it is important to pick the right questions that the strategy attempts to answer. Though there is no universal set, it may be useful to build your transformation strategy around the following, with the overarching goal of achieving a sustained competitive advantage.

- **Market differentiation:** How will I create clear market differentiation through digital innovation?
- **Customer loyalty:** How can the application of enhanced digital tools help me improve customer experience through the life cycle?
- **Cost reduction:** How can I achieve better productivity and asset management with digital technology?
- **Operational efficiency:** How can I achieve efficiency gains in operations and service delivery through digital transformation?
- **Agility, speed-to-market:** How do I leverage digital technology to optimize my business processes for higher agility and speed-to-market?

## Refresh Your Information Technology Charter

The IT function and its leadership in a digital enterprise can no longer be defined only by their ability to manage crises, maintain IT assets, and efficiently *run* the operations. Digital transformation calls for an IT leadership and organization that can realign the IT people, processes, technology, and information to *transform* (change) the business creatively and consultatively. In a digital enterprise, IT is an equal stakeholder in the creation of business value, and this must reflect in the renewed IT charter, which should now include:

- Accountability for the business outcome
- Ownership of the customer experience

- Developing the plan and capability for new technology platforms in line with the business roadmap
- Future-proofing the business
- Thought leadership

## Design an Adaptable IT Architecture for the Digital Business

Digital business requires a very resilient and robust foundational IT platform, on which new services may easily and quickly be constructed to achieve targeted business outcomes. **Enterprise Architecture** (EA) is best adapted for digital business as it improves organizational impacts through productivity, agility, product and service timeliness, revenue growth, and cost reduction.[8] The essential aspect here is that various business services can be dynamically reconfigured to suit the changing landscape of the digital enterprise.

## Develop the Right Structure for Digital Business

For a digital enterprise, the mindsets and competencies required for success are quite different from traditional enterprises. People need to reinvent themselves, and those ensconced in tight comfort zones often do not find a place. It is essential to onboard people who, apart from being competent in their core function, are

- Customer-centric to the point of obsession
- Continuously looking to innovate
- Agile (quick to change), data-driven, challengers of status quo
- Business folks with a strong aptitude for technology
- IT folks with a strong aptitude for business

Digital transformation requires a strong leader with ownership and authority to make changes in the organization, implement current and future digital initiatives, and own the customer experience. This leader may be from the Technology or Business/Marketing organization, with a clear focus on digital strategy that goes beyond functional boundaries.

### Boost Your BITA Power as You Prepare Your Digital Launch

The stage is now set for your launch into the digital space. At this juncture, a strong BITA could be a shot-in-the-arm for enterprises. As you construct the digital edifice, Business and IT must take calls on the legacy systems to be retained, revamped, or retired, as well as the future systems to be developed or acquired, considering both the business and technology implications. Also, while the transformation is underway, Business and IT must work interdependently in an agile, iterative cycle to deliver an enhanced user experience as they shape the enterprise's digital future. Without this functional harmony, or alignment, between Business and IT the transformation could be an exercise in futility. BITA is, therefore, the backbone of digital transformation and early benefits to customers.

The best time to start, if you haven't already, is *now*. Run the transformation as your highest priority project with clearly defined milestones and a system of measuring the progress in your journey. Companies that get their project blueprint "bought-in" by all stakeholders early in terms of deliverables, schedule, and funding have the best chance of executing it successfully.

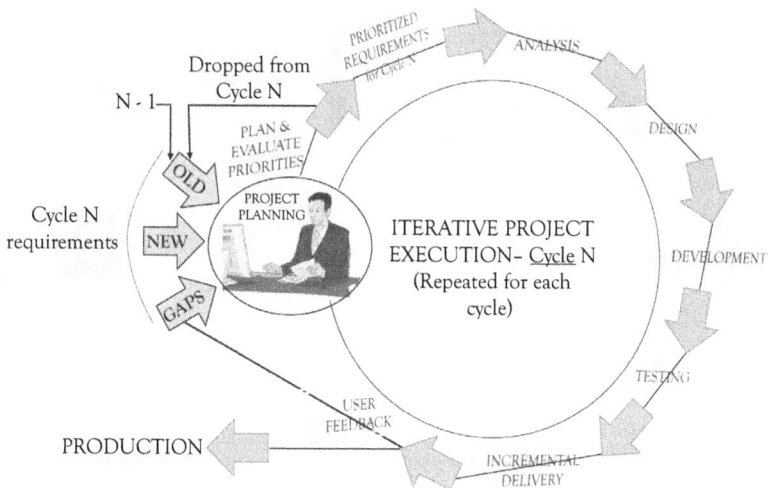

*Figure 4.4 Iterative project execution cycle*

A digital transformation project is run in an agile or iterative mode. This means that it must factor in frequent changes in business requirements, as opposed to a traditional (*waterfall*) project where all requirements are frozen *before* the project kicks off, and the next stage only starts when the previous one ends. That is, a flexible approach, which allows for *incremental* deliveries, is best suited for digital transformation. This also helps with fine-tuning the output by feeding any quality or performance gaps back into the next-stage requirements. It is beyond this book to go into the description of the iterative project methodology, but a conceptual drawing is presented here (Figure 4.4) for context.

The agile model, which is based on continuous feedback and interaction between users and executors, reduces uncertainty in the final delivery, though there is often some confusion initially with less clarity on precisely what must be prioritized for delivery (Figure 4.5).

While we have touched on a few essential aspects of transforming to a digital enterprise, let me reemphasize here that digital transformation does *not* happen by merely adopting new technology. You may implement the most advanced technologies but would still not become a digital enterprise unless the entire organization transforms itself to take

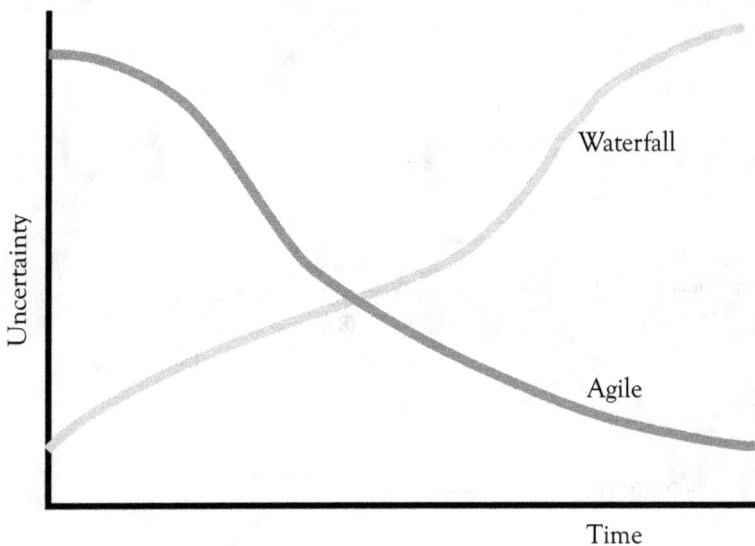

*Figure 4.5 Project uncertainty*

advantage of the potential unleashed by these new technologies. It's a bit like putting the latest smartphone in the hands of your grandmother and expecting her to exploit its full potential even while she is happy with her button-phone and does not aspire to anything beyond! It's the same for enterprises—*people must be ready first.*

There are many great examples of successful digital transformation by companies. I had an opportunity to meet with some of the transformation champions, mostly the Chief Information Officer (CIO), Chief Marketing Officer (CMO), or Chief Digital Officer (CDO), at organizations that have successfully transformed their businesses and it was inspiring to hear them speak very passionately about their experiences. They all spoke of the eight steps that we described earlier. Here are some of the other lessons shared by almost all of them:

1. The ultimate goal of digital transformation is an unwavering connection with the customer.
2. Digital transformation depends heavily on a *shared* passion for achieving the company's vision.
3. It is a journey that takes new turns every day, opening up exciting possibilities. And challenges.
4. It does *not* require doing away with your existing IT infrastructure, though some consolidation must be done. In fact, it was now possible to get *more* out of this infra than ever before.
5. Listening to the younger generation has been very useful in deriving innovative insights. Most large companies are not doing this enough.
6. Engaging an external transformation consultant helps, but only as a conscience keeper and facilitator. The real impetus comes from the passion shared by the entire workforce.
7. Alignment between Business and IT was never a greater need than it is during and after the transformation. It must be built and nurtured as an asset.

**Example 4.4**

*One of the leading wall paint companies in India has had a very remarkable metamorphosis from a manufacturing company to a digital service enterprise. Of course, it still manufactures but at the core now is its renewed vision to improve the experience of its retailers and customers at every touchpoint, using digital technology. The company's retailers can now devote quality time to helping customers, rather than sort transactional issues internally. Customers have also been given a choice to browse product catalogs on the web and make their selections at home, where the paint is to be applied in the end, instead of at the retail shop. Retailers can submit their customers' orders digitally through a centralized call center, allowing faster fulfillment by tapping into the many depots scattered across the country. This also frees up the company's salespeople from the cumbersome and time-consuming order collection and fulfillment process. The salespeople leveraged Mobility by adopting tablet devices so that relevant information is always available at their fingertips. The company expects customer loyalty as well as the demand to get a boost through this initiative, which, in turn, will reflect in a healthier balance sheet, and an edge over the competition.*

*The company achieved all this through a transformation of its core IT systems and processes, which included the implementation of a B2B portal, cloud-based CRM and Enterprise Resource Planning (ERP), mobility, and analytics tools. The digital transformation enabled the company to sell services instead of products—a complete shift in the business model and market positioning. Instead of selling a can of paint, it now offers the service of a painted wall. This enables them to better meet customer requirements, including guidance to customers on the proper application of higher-end products. The company could also better understand customer preferences and potential demand, which helped create more targeted offerings. The benefits are many and varied and go much beyond revenue. Importantly, now there is a direct engagement of the end-customer in the product-planning process. Traditionally, end-customer involvement in the paints (or most manufactured goods) business was very low. Digital has changed that.*

*The above called for a high degree of commitment to a shared goal by all parts of the company. Without the passionate participation of all stakeholders, a transformation of this kind would remain a vision. We find in this example that all the steps we spoke about—most importantly, the transformation of IT systems and processes in tune with a change in the business model—have been applied.*

The world of digital business is a lot different from our familiar world of traditional (or *analog*) business. The quirks of the digital world would be unimaginable a few years ago. Uber is the largest taxi service in the world, though it does not own a single car. Skype provides one of the world's largest communication services without owning a single piece of telecom infra! Some of the world's biggest retailers, like Alibaba, hold no merchandise in their inventories. Even the world's largest movie house, Netflix, does not own or run a single cinema. Facebook does not create content, yet it is one of the largest media owners on the planet today. If it's not capital or infrastructure, what has powered the phenomenal rise of these—and many other—successful digital enterprises? The answer lies in focusing on the *interface* rather than the *product*, and the ability to leverage technology for business in very innovative ways to weave a reality around an idea that became a vision for the enterprise. Enterprises that have institutionalized BITA have a clear edge.

Before we go into measuring and improving specific dimensions of BITA for your organization, let us look at the results of a survey that was conducted among folks from various organizations on the digital path, and discover the relative importance and role of BITA in influencing enterprise success. This is the topic of the following chapter.

# CHAPTER 5

# BITA: An Outside-In View

While few would still doubt the need and importance of Business–Technology (or IT) alignment (BITA) in the new economy, gaining an insider perspective on BITA from a cross-section of viewpoints may be a credible barometer to ascertain its place among the myriad of concerns and priorities afflicting a typical enterprise. In the earlier chapters, we discussed the evolution of BITA as a driver of enterprise success in the digital age. Now let us look at how some real organizations view BITA and the factors influencing it.

I approached a select but insightful set of people from both Business and Technology backgrounds with a simple questionnaire seeking their views on critical factors influencing business in the digital economy. This set was constituted of folks from different industries. The individuals contacted were from the senior and middle management rungs of Business and IT streams in organizations that have already made deep digital inroads (Figure 5.1).

In this chapter, I am presenting a consolidated view of the responses received. Given the profiles of the people who responded I consider this a reasonably accurate and tenable assessment, which can be extrapolated to represent a credible picture. I have only considered responses from individuals who are deeply associated with driving digital initiatives and have achieved a certain degree of success in their ventures.

The charts simply rank the various attributes in their order of importance as scored by the respondents, and there is no attempt to slice and dice the data to derive inferences which may be open to interpretation. I am presenting the questionnaire that was used in this survey later in the chapter, and I encourage you to run this among the key people in your

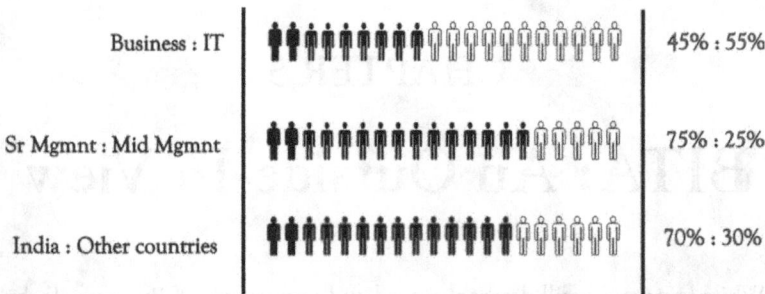

| | | |
|---|---|---|
| Business : IT | | 45% : 55% |
| Sr Mgmnt : Mid Mgmnt | | 75% : 25% |
| India : Other countries | | 70% : 30% |

*Figure 5.1  Survey respondents*

organization to create similar charts for your unit. This may provide some useful tips that may help as you work your way up.

These charts are not intended as a rigid benchmark to be necessarily aspired by your organization. They are statistical derivations. At best, they can provide you broad guidelines. Your individual situation may well be different and yet be good. That said, I do believe that if you are reading this book, you probably place a high importance on BITA. If the results of the survey sharply contradict this view, you may like to mull over this and prepare a plan to pull it up.

## What Creates Market Differentiation?

The first part of the survey was to determine the critical differentiators in the new economy. Surprisingly, the usual suspects that one would associate with differentiation in the old economy, namely speed, brand (reputation), service, and pricing also emerged among the top differentiators in the new economy. Features like geography/coverage and logistics were considered too tactical (and location-specific) while people practices and ethical business conduct were considered too foundational to be included and hence were dropped from the list. In the end, we had six key items, which included three *new* entrants: *innovative offerings* (which encompassed a dare-to-try spirit), *customer experience* (which replaced customer service) and of course, *Business–IT Alignment* (which as we saw did not figure in any significant way in determining the course of business in the old economy).

The respondents, from both Business and IT streams, were asked to give a score of 1–10 against each of the six attributes in terms of its potential for creating market differentiation, 1 being no-impact-at-all and progressively increasing in order of importance up to a maximum of 10. It may be noted that the responses here are from an *internal* company view and not the end-customer perspective (Figure 5.2).

As with all surveys, we did get some surprises. For example, consistency and quality of *customer experience* were rated significantly higher by the Business than by IT in terms of its potential for creating market differentiation. While IT may consider customer experience a *hygiene* factor, Business places higher importance on this attribute as a *market differentiator*. On the other hand, IT puts higher emphasis than Business on *speed-to-market*, at least in spirit. Whether it gets translated into aggressive delivery schedules is not clear from the survey, but at the very least, this points to a heightened sense of urgency in IT to deliver quickly.

It is no surprise that innovative offerings is rated as the most critical differentiator in a rapidly changing business world, which is increasingly dominated by technology. Business–IT alignment is ranked as the third most important factor for creating market differentiation in the new economy, coming narrowly after customer experience. In my view, this says a lot about the pace at which the contribution of technology functions in ensuring business success has grown in a few quick years.

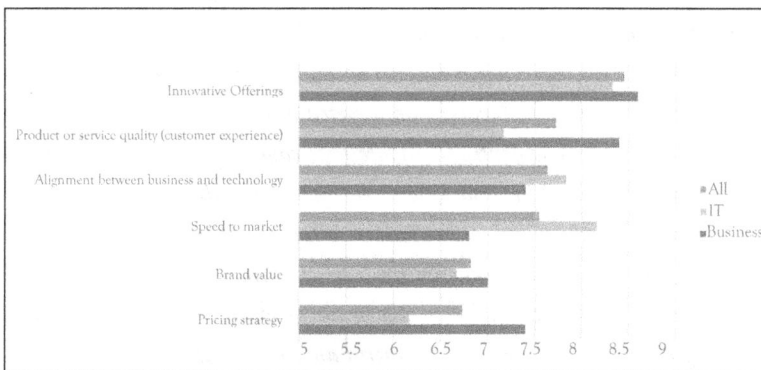

*Figure 5.2 What creates market differentiation in the new economy*

**Example 5.1**

*The power of BITA to create market differentiation is a lot more pronounced in the new economy as IT-enabled solutions like Big data and mobility have come to rule the business landscape. One of the respondents to the survey, a banker, had an interesting tale to exemplify this. The bank being referred to is a large financial institution (FI) providing personal banking, insurance, home loans, and credit cards for the individual customer and a host of merchant banking services for business enterprises. The various units of this FI, however, might as well have been different companies, for there was no common denominator in their operations. The customers of one unit were complete strangers to the other units. There was no common thread that tied together the experiences across different units. Someone who had availed a home loan from this FI and expected to be recognized, let alone be rewarded, when they took insurance for their car was in for a big disappointment. Other than earning the displeasure of the customers, this was also causing the bank to miss out on a substantial cross-selling opportunity. Everyone knew about this problem, but the cry that rang through the portals was a dismissive "what can we do?"*

*This issue eventually came up in one of the board meetings, and it was decided to take a crack at the problem. The leaders of the IT and Business units were summoned. As a first step, a central governing group was created, tasked not with operations but with identifying cross-unit potentialities. The group focused on amalgamating information (transaction records) of the last three years from different units. The intelligence gathered was instrumental in grouping customers into demographic segments to support sales and campaigns across units. This was achieved by analyzing all the amassed data using Big data analytics.*

*The close interworking between the Business and IT teams did not end here. The teams next worked on targeted product and service offerings to customers by implementing software that could segment the customers based on their preferences and history. The system was also open to inputs in the form of social media feeds to analyze customer sentiments and opinions and identify key influencers across the lines of business.*

*These actions generated a visible wave of excitement and optimism among the internal stakeholders, which I am sure was shared by customers approaching the bank for different types of services.*

BITA is the hidden force that is behind many a success story in the digital economy. Even a relatively simple project, like putting a new feature or changing the user interface on a mobile application, run collaboratively between customer teams and IT could produce vastly different business results. I am therefore entirely in agreement with our survey on the high importance of BITA as a factor for creating clear market differentiation. Are you?

## Why Does Business–IT Alignment Matter?

There was a consensus among folks I met that BITA mattered in the new economy. But *why* did it matter? What were the expected outcomes of BITA? We agreed on a set of reasons as the motivations for enterprises to embrace BITA and asked the respondents to score them on a similar scale of 1 to 10, where 1 signified the least impact of BITA and 10 signified maximum impact. There were wider variations between Business and IT on this question, but both agreed overwhelmingly that the effect of BITA on *improving customer experience* was the highest. No surprises here. Overall, Business was more upbeat on the impact of BITA on almost all the selected parameters than IT. Significantly, the old-economy attribute of cost control ranked the lowest among the motivations for embracing BITA, and on this specific parameter, there was a very close agreement between Business and IT. This does not mean that cost optimization is *not* expected to result from BITA, but that it is not the primary reason people are embracing Business–IT alignment within their organizations (Figure 5.3).

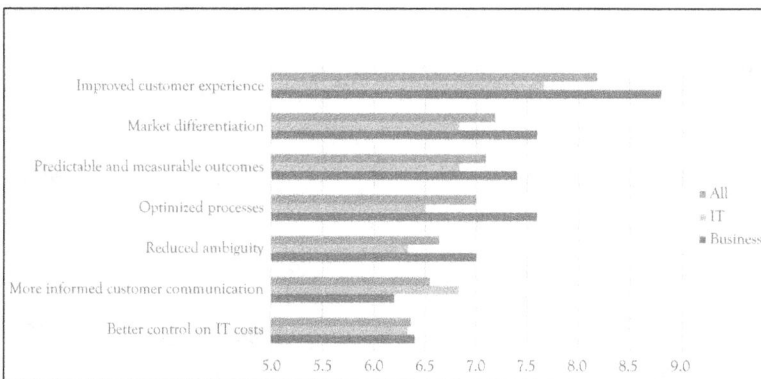

*Figure 5.3 Why does Business-IT alignment matter*

## Example 5.2

*This incident was narrated by a senior IT Project Manager from a very reputed software services firm (let's call it SSF), who participated in the BITA survey. A year ago, one of their U.S. clients had visited their development facilities in India to evaluate SSF for a new project. SSF was one of the four shortlisted companies whose centers were being visited by the client team during the week. The day started at 10 a.m. with the arrival of the client at the facilities where the traditional Indian welcome of garlanding and lamp lighting was accorded. The client team was cordially escorted into the swanky facilities, which had a space-age conference room laden with refreshments of a wide variety. No detail was overlooked, however trivial. The client team, led by the director of engineering, was here introduced to the top leadership of SSF, which brimmed with an eagerness to serve and an unshakeable bonhomie. After this, the client team patiently sat through some impressive PowerPoints on SSF's people and processes, success rate, client testimonials, the works.*

*After lunch, which was sumptuous, the client made an unexpected request which threatened to deviate the proceedings from the choreographed routine. This client had recently acquired another company (let's call it AC2), which was also a client of SSF. The director of the client company asked if they could visit the dedicated development center that SSF ran for AC2 and interact with the team members there. Some murmurs ensued regarding lack of notice, client security, and confidentiality but in the end, the request was ceded.*

*What followed was an exemplary show of conduct that brought a major twist to the story. As the client team walked into the AC2 delivery center, which had not been alerted formally, there were some mildly curious glances, but otherwise, it was business as usual. The director of the client team stopped at a corner desk where a young lady was contemplatively sitting at a workstation with two screens. He spoke to her directly. Asked her first about who she was, her experience, and role in the project. It turned out she was two years out of college and was an Associate Software Engineer assigned to the AC2 project. The client asked her a series of questions relating to the project and how her work fit into the larger picture. She gave a detailed and accurate answer to each question and spoke about AC2 the company, its mission, the various touchpoints, and the processes for staying in sync on the deliverables and dates. As the client later confided, he was completely taken in by this young engineer's in-depth and contextual understanding of not only the project, but the business of AC2, perhaps beyond her designated charter, and this swung the deal in SSF's favor.*

*All the sales and marketing effort, swanky facilities, affirmations of top management, and impressive track record of SSF were rendered trivial before this display of close alignment of the company's engineering (Technology) function with the customer's business, which was apparent at the working level. As the customer wrote later in his testimonial, "The sense of urgency that the SSF team displayed across the board not only fixed problems for us quickly but prevented a lot of them from surfacing. This team worked with minimal supervision and knew exactly what our customers expected. We had no hesitation at all in going back to them when we embarked on our expansion project lately." The grandest sales effort can only bring the customer to your door. However, an emotional connect that culminates in building a long-term relationship is squarely the preserve of BITA.*

The impact of pervasive BITA in influencing the customer's overall perception of the company is apparent here. Regardless of the size and nature of your business, *BITA is your best bet* in the digital economy.

## What Drives BITA in an Organization?

The third question of the survey was directed at determining the factors that need to be institutionalized in an organization aspiring to a high BITA. In arriving at the list of choices, we excluded intangibles like mindsets, Business/IT competence, attitudes, and situational behaviors, simply to retain objectivity in the evaluation, and not because they are considered any less important for BITA. In the following chapter, we will introduce the seven dimensions that cover all aspects that matter for BITA. In the book *Mastering the 7 Dimensions of Business–Technology Alignment*[1] by the same author, their ramifications are discussed in greater detail.

The agreement between Business and IT was the closest in this question, on almost all the listed factors (Figure 5.4). Both Business and IT gave equal importance to *leadership example and role modeling* as the factor with the maximum potential to enhance BITA in the organization. It is indeed hard to imagine a BITA-powered environment under a listless

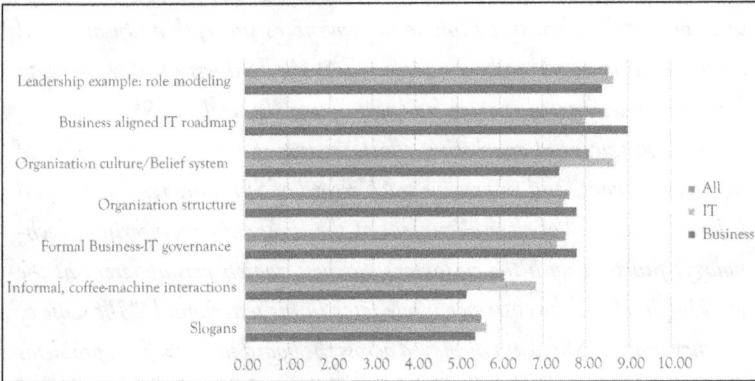

*Figure 5.4* **What drives BITA in an organization**

leadership. As we have said before, BITA must be driven from the top, reinforced at every possible opportunity, and led by example.

Closely following this, and entirely on expected lines, was *Business-aligned IT roadmap*. All it takes to arrive at the best IT roadmap is to use the business strategy as its foundation and include Business in the preparation. The most common, and frequently overlooked, reason for business failure in the new economy is an IT roadmap that is not supportive of future needs of the business.

*The Digital India movement is a case in point for illustrating the impact of leadership example and role modeling. India has a growing necessity to streamline the availability of government services to its citizens, through digitization and high-speed Internet connectivity, which the Digital India project aims to provide, particularly to large sections of the deprived population in rural areas. The DI project also envisages rendering broader market access, e-health, and e-banking services to millions, which would benefit communities through higher empowerment, and finally an opportunity to reskill the youth to drive digital literacy and create more options for employment. All in all, Digital India project is firmly on the critical path of India's progress.*

*It was only on being articulated and reinforced by the top leadership of the country—no less than the Prime Minister—that the rubber hit the road. If the PM and his senior ministers did not emphasize this initiative at every available opportunity, driving home its advantages to all and sundry, the project would have been a nonstarter. As I write this, a lot is taking shape on this front. I hope to see in my lifetime the benefits of this program reach all parts of the country, including its most disadvantaged sections, bringing about a significant and measurable improvement in the quality-of-life index and the level of empowerment enjoyed by all. The most significant factor behind its eventual success would undoubtedly be the role of the country's leadership in focusing the attention of the government machinery, industry bodies, institutes of learning, and the common man alike to make this a personal mission.*

If leadership example and role modeling can energize a nation of 1.30 billion, think of what it can do for your organization, which has a much higher proportion of highly erudite folks routinely achieving the impossible! A spark from the leadership would go much farther in igniting the fire of digital transformation across your organization. Unfortunately, the converse is also true. The fire would fail to conflagrate *without* that spark, and the enterprise would quickly degenerate into cold embers, only useful for future case studies that caution against following its example.

**Survey Questionnaire** (As it was sent to respondents)

In the current times, the importance of Business-IT alignment cannot be overemphasized. I would like to collect some views on important aspects around Business-IT alignment for an important project that I am working on. I need your help on a few basic questions on this topic, which would help me immensely in presenting a well-rounded view on the subject.

In this respect, I would greatly appreciate if you could take a couple of minutes out whenever convenient to quickly respond to the below. **The response is purely numeric. You only need to put a number between 1 and 10 against each line, that is, give marks out of 10,** based on your judgment/ experience.

(1 is least in importance, 10 is highest in importance)

1. Rate each of the following on a scale of 1-10 on their potential for creating market differentiation in the Digital Age
   - Speed to market
   - Pricing strategy
   - Innovative offerings
   - Product/Service quality
   - Brand value
   - Alignment between Business and Technology (IT)
2. Why does Business-IT Alignment matter? Rate each of the following from 1-10 as a motive for improving Business-IT alignment
   - Market differentiation
   - Improved customer experience
   - Better control on IT Costs
   - More informed customer communication
   - Optimized processes
   - Predictable and measurable outcomes
3. What is the importance of each of the following in attaining a strong level of Business-IT alignment (Rate each on 1-10)
   - Organization structure
   - Organization belief system

- Leadership example/Role-modeling ☐
- Formal Business–IT governance structure ☐
- Informal, coffee-machine interactions ☐
- Business-aligned IT roadmap ☐
- Slogans ☐

4. In your view where would your company be today on its Business-IT alignment index (1-10)? ☐

5. What is a realistic target level of alignment after one year for you (1-10) ☐

This is for statistical analysis only, and all responses will be treated in strictest confidence. Still, if you choose not to answer any question, it is fine.

I value your opinion and hence seeking it.

Thanks in advance,

Ashish

The survey form and analysis tool can also be downloaded from www,alignedtowin.com

# CHAPTER 6

# What's Your BITA Level?

In Chapter 2, we briefly looked at some of the characteristics that enterprises striving for higher Business–Technology alignment (BITA) need to possess and display. The question, however, is how *you* as an enterprise stack up on the BITA scale. While BITA is not a purely numeric entity—much like your quality or customer-centricity attribute—it is possible to get a fair idea of your BITA level through a simple tool that I am now introducing. Of course, the ultimate evidence of a strong BITA is the success you achieve in the digital marketplace through the joint efforts of Business and Technology. Nonetheless, some preparatory guidance in determining your BITA level as well as gaps may prove helpful in focusing on the right attributes for capitalizing on the digital opportunity around you.

It is essential to go into the individual components of BITA to ascertain where to put your emphasis for better alignment between Business and Technology. In this chapter, we will introduce the seven dimensions of BITA and a way to measure how you stack up on each dimension. As with any tool, the composition of the users and the integrity with which responses are provided will be critical factors in determining the accuracy of results.

## The Seven Dimensions for BITA

We noted in the previous chapter that Business–Technology alignment is rated among the most important success factors for a digital enterprise. Ascertaining your position on the BITA scale will help assess your success chances in the world of digital business and allow you to focus on the right attributes for enhancing your prospects. The BITA calculator introduced here helps you do precisely this, by simply evaluating your responses to a set of statements.

In a trial run of the BITA calculator, I found that people equate BITA very tightly to the overall digital transformation status of the enterprise. While this may well turn out to be true in many cases, it is important to remember that BITA is only *one*, albeit significant, attribute of a successful digital enterprise among several others. BITA is the ideal starting point of the inevitable journey you must embark upon to digitally transform your enterprise.

Business–IT alignment refers to aligning at seven different levels, or *dimensions*. Before we move to the tool-based assessment of BITA Index, let us briefly study each of its dimensions. The term "dimension" is used here to define each critical factor that matters in the attainment of BITA. It is important to note that just like our spatial dimensions (Length, Breadth, Height), these are *all* equally required for creating a solid, durable model. Figure 6.1 shows the seven dimensions of BITA, which are

BITA EQUALS ALIGNMENT AT THE LEVEL OF:

*Figure 6.1 The seven dimensions of Business–IT alignment*

applicable across various industries and business segments, enabling uniform benchmarking.

Each of the dimensions is the subject of detailed treatment in the next book in this series, *Mastering the 7 Dimensions of Business–Technology Alignment.*[1] However, a quick primer and some pointers (features that give evidence of the dimension being ingrained in the organization) of the individual dimensions are being included here for quick and ready reference.

## Cultural Alignment

Cultural alignment implies that the people in Business and Technology consciously, consistently, and collectively live by the same set of values, principles, norms, and code of conduct, frequently emanating from the organization's *belief system*, in their actions, words, and behavior. Some pointers:

- Well-articulated belief system
- Shared vision, driven from the top
- Result orientation (focus on the outcome)
- Drive for excellence
- Customer centricity
- Transparency and openness
- Continuous learning and development
- Intolerance of mediocrity

---

**Example 6.1**

*A diversified and well-established family business was known for the sharp division between its top management and the rest of the organization. There were separate elevators, floors, cafeterias, and even restrooms for the top brass. Disdain and contempt were the norm. The pay was good and jobs scarce, so no one thought about things like employee morale. When this company decided, or rather was compelled, to go digital, it hired expensive consultants and kept aside a fat budget for technology acquisition. However, it faced two problems. One, they had to work with partners and contractors who expected courtesy and indiscrimination. Two, they had to hire young folks with a different work ethos and outlook. Neither could blend in with the company's culture. The management went through some behavioral programs to learn the new ropes. However, years of pomposity cannot be washed off quickly. They could not rally the team behind a shared digital vision, nor usher in a culture of alignment, both prerequisites to successful digital transformation. The management's arrogance often flashed through the pretense. Within months, their new joiners left the company, and it lost the reputation it had built over years. Soon they had no one left to carry the digital torch. The group that had thrived for half a century faded away in less than two years, only due to its inability to adjust to the new cultural climate.*

Culture is what defines the company, and it's *not* invisible. Even if an outcome is positive, culture (behavior) can negate it. Culture emanates from a shared belief system, reinforced by the management in words and action at every opportunity.

## Strategic Alignment

Strategic alignment is about Business and Technology deriving their goals and plans from a *shared mission*, which is to make the business successful. Some pointers:

- Understanding of business strategy at *all* levels of the organization
- IT Architecture and technology roadmap alignment with business strategy
- Correspondence between Technology KRAs and Business strategy
- Flexibility to respond to market changes
- Shared mission and vision for the company

- Technology readiness to support the future needs of the business

Creating the right business strategy is almost certainly the most impactful aspect of running a business. A strategy that is incongruent with your core competency could be an open invitation to disaster. It is vital that the business strategy is communicated clearly to all constituents, including Technology teams. The technology strategy must evolve from the business strategy.

---

**Example 6.2**

*It is quite common to build a strategy around adjacencies, like finding new products for existing markets or finding new markets for existing products. Nothing wrong with that, but it requires a lot of preparatory work at all levels. If done hastily, it could spell disaster for even your existing line of business. A telecom services company bet big on its foray into software development services, banking on its reputation (as a telco) to attract exceptional talent, and on its relationships with OEMs to attract business for its new venture. Even with all the investment in getting people on-boarded, setting up facilities, and so on, the venture never really took off. Instead of relying on a strategic fit, the group had entered the venture on the assumption of quid pro quo deals with telecom OEMs. The core competence required for this venture was quite different from the proven skills it had in its mainstream telco business. To top that, there were established players who could do software development jobs better and cheaper. The company lost money and goodwill, which made survival difficult. Apparently, the business strategy here was out of sync with the core competence and brand positioning. On perhaps a smaller scale, this is what happens when the technology roadmap does not support our business plan. Incidentally, the above company later revamped its mission and strategy to reinvent itself as a developer of software products for telecom service providers globally—a field much better aligned to its parent core competence—and achieved a turnaround to become a prime acquisition target of its larger competitors. The lesson here is that it may never be too late in the journey to invest in aligning your business strategy and the technology roadmap, even if you have suffered some knocks en route.*

---

# Structural Alignment

Structural alignment is the attainment of synergy in the *organization* and *responsibilities* of Business and IT teams, that lead them to think, build, and operate together for achieving their shared mission. Some pointers:

- Business-led IT organization
- Core competence defined and built
- Clear roles and responsibilities
- Unambiguous interfaces between Business and Technology
- Think, build, and operate together
- Skills aligned with business direction
- Flexibility to adapt technology skills to changing business needs

Structural alignment has a lot to do with collaborative interworking leading to Business and Technology complementing each other effectively and always. It is not only about creating congruent organization structures and reporting paths but, as we often observe in team sports, building synergy and solidarity leading to greater strength. Its absence achieves the opposite, as this example illustrates.

---

**Example 6.3**

*As engineering director at my company's delivery center in Bangalore, India, I once submitted a proposal in response to a customer inquiry from Texas in the United States. In a few weeks, I learned that our proposal had been accepted and that the customer had invited our company for the technical round. I traveled all the way from Bangalore to Dallas, fully prepared to present our technical proposal and to answer all potential questions that may come from the customer on our approach and methodology. When the questions started after the presentation, however, I was in for a surprise. These questions were not directed at my colleagues or me. Instead, these were directed at the customer's own Technology team from their Business folks! The questions were about their (the customer's) current technology capability, the share of ownership between Business and Technology, business benefits of the project, budgetary approvals for the project, staff availability for managing the project, and the like. Obviously, the two functions rarely met and had no common interfaces. It almost became a scuffle between the customer's internal teams. We were simply mute, and somewhat embarrassed, spectators. The most surprising part was that this proposed project, for which we had submitted our partnering bid to this company, was to develop a solution for this company's biggest global customer! How would this company meet the expectations of its customer in the face of such apparent misalignment between its own Business and Technology arms? As it turned out, it didn't have to, as the end-customer scrapped the project which I strongly suspect was due to lack of a cohesive response from its existing supplier. You will probably find several such examples around you, without having to traverse the globe!*

## Process (or Procedural) Alignment

Procedural alignment is the synchronization between Business and Technology on the enterprise processes, tools, and methods with a view to achieving shared outcomes while avoiding conflicting, uncoordinated activities. Some pointers:

- Simple, flexible, adaptable processes
- Customer-centric business processes
- Tools adoption (automation)
- Focus on continuous improvement
- Change management
- Process innovation
- Instinctual connect

Process alignment is about assuring that the technology delivery and operations processes in the organization stay tuned to the *changing* needs of the business. The *processes* must align with the business and *not* the other way. Nothing blunts your edge more than processes that remain static in a dynamic business world. This is also evidence of poor change management. It is particularly true of *automated* processes which are considered the holy grail in many companies and trump customer experience. Here's an example of how some inflexible processes may cost the business.

---

**Example 6.4**

*Late one night, I arrived at the hotel I routinely stay in during my frequent business trips to a city in India. I was a proud owner of this hotel chain's loyalty card. As always, I had a room reservation, and my secretary had duly printed out the reservation confirmation page, which I was carrying. I was shocked, therefore, when the gent at the front desk, after welcoming me back with a cheery smile, informed me that I had no reservation. I protested this and showed him the confirmation sheet. The manager was summoned, and investigations started while I was asked to wait in the lobby. After a seemingly interminable period, the manager came to me, having the triumphant expression of a man who has just solved a big mystery. It turned out there was a group of four other executives from my company scheduled to check in that evening, and a few hours ago they had canceled their booking. Their system, which was designed to put all guests from a company in one bracket, automatically changed my Confirmed status to "Wait-list: PAX Advice pending" as per some apparently goofy logic and sent an auto intimation to the booking agent (after office hours apparently). The hotel manager meanwhile was visibly relieved as it was a big problem off his chest. After all, it was a process issue, not his doing. Where in the world does one question an auto process? No, he said, I couldn't be confirmed as there were no longer any rooms available that night, due to that IT expo happening in the city! It was now midnight. I managed something elsewhere at a rate beyond my approved limit, feeling very disgruntled at the treatment. I made sure that no one from my organization ever used this hotel again. I do hope my experience triggered a change in that hotel's process though I am not going back to find out! Process automation is well and good but cannot substitute the application of common sense!*

---

## Intellectual Alignment

Intellectual alignment refers to Business and Technology being on the same intellectual plane to drive technological *innovation* without fear of failure for the realization of their shared transformation goals. Some pointers:

- Spirit of innovation—Incentivizing ideas and daring to try
- Exploiting new technology for competitive advantage
- Tracking new trends and piloting their adoption for business advantage
- Differentiated products and services
- Customer feedback-driven tech innovation
- Future readiness of IT architecture and capabilities

Intellectual alignment occurs when Business and Technology have the consensus, conviction, and empowerment to apply *innovation* for the enhancement of business value. It goes beyond demonstrating *technical competence,* to breaking the confines of established practices and daring to be different. Kodak's inability to recognize the market potential of digital photography, which it *invented,* is a well-known and classic example of intellectual misalignment leading to a great company's downfall.

---

**Example 6.5**

*Kodak moments may be more common than you think.[9] In 1995, Alta Vista launched the first Internet Search but ended up setting the stage for Google, dying a rather slow and unceremonious death. BlackBerry devices were the first smartphones for many users, able to connect to the Internet, send and receive e-mail, and chat with one another over the company's BlackBerry Messenger, or BBM, service. And they were everywhere. However, it stuck too long with its proprietary design, yielding to full touch-screen phones like the iPhone. Apple's digital newspaper, The Daily, failed in the first two years despite great graphics and embedded video, due to an unsustainable business model. AOL, the first Internet service provider in the United States and the first with an Instant Messenger service, lost an excellent opportunity to lead the social networking revolution to smaller but smarter players. The Palm Pilot was the first mainstream digital hand-held (1997) to capture public imagination, but in spite of selling over a million units in its first year, and pioneering mobile computing,*

> *it never made it as a smartphone. There are many other tragic stories like these—Netscape, Segway, and Napster being a few others. All the above were great innovations but were not backed by a strong enough conviction (backbone) that they could make it as leaders. Innovation takes a lot more than ingenuity.*

## Functional Alignment

Functional alignment between Business and Technology is the overcoming of functional barriers (silos) to harmonize the priorities that drive their decisions, measurements, and actions. Some pointers:

- Measurement of business value of IT
- Collaborative prospecting, presales, fulfillment, and delivery
- Business-led IT funding
- Business-outcome driven IT delivery and operations
- Quick time to market
- Success of digital initiatives (like marketing campaigns)

Functional alignment leads to *business-outcome-based IT,* which we touched upon in Chapter 2 with examples from a few sectors. The simple example below goes to demonstrate how unwise it is to base the function's measurement system on a set of attributes that have almost no bearing on business results.

---

**Example 6.6**

*John D\* was the head of the customer support operations for an independent business unit that produced peripherals, mainly printers, for computer systems. John's internal stakeholders were clearly interested in metrics that provided useful information for them to act upon. For example, the Factory wanted to know the number and nature of defective arrivals which they could use to crank up the QA processes. The Business wanted to know about the life expectancy of the print head or cartridge so that they could plan their consumables sales accordingly. They would have also liked some*

---

*benchmark data on usage trends and the customers' overall satisfaction with the product. However, what John's team did regularly present to the Business (and Factory) was data on the total backlog of complaints in Sev 1/2/3, average response and turnaround time for complaints, number of calls handled per engineer (productivity), and so on. Only after this had been going on for a couple of years, someone finally broke through the silos to say that it was serving no practical purpose to anyone outside John's team. John's priorities were evidently mismatched with those of the stakeholders. Had he indeed ascertained and acted on the needs and preferences of the business and focused on the outcome instead of internal attributes, the company would easily have a higher competitive ranking. As it were, they finished fifth among six players! This example is a wake-up call to IT organizations that are inward focused as opposed to outcome-oriented. Any amount of introspection in hindsight is futile – reevaluate your measurement systems today and tune them to the business priorities.*

* Not his real name, of course.

## Tactical Alignment

Tactical alignment refers to step-locking for *executing* on the joint strategy through a supportive *service, operations,* and *delivery infrastructure* designed to ensure an outstanding *customer experience* consistently. Some pointers:

- Collaborative project delivery and execution
- Supportive Technology infrastructure (e.g., digital platform)
- Shared ownership of customer experience through the lifecycle
- Excellence in technology operations and services

For much of their histories, Business and Technology have followed diverse tactical paths. The convergence, if any, ended with the overlap of certain items of strategy but as far as tactics were concerned, it was each to his own. The advent of the digital era has changed that. You cannot, for example, launch an app-based product strategy (say a taxi service) without Business and Technology intricately collaborating at every step of the development and operations. Tactical alignment implies that Business and IT are complementing each other in the execution of their digital strategy for delivering a superior experience to their customer throughout the lifecycle.

---

**Example 6.7**

*A telecom operator was banking on an innovative product that marketing research had shown would be hugely impactful in consolidating its lead. The CIO was steering the development project. One evening, while in a hotel room, the CIO was startled to see his company's ad on the TV announcing the availability of the product to the market two weeks earlier than the scheduled date! Though this was the original launch date, it had been extended in the project plan due to some new requirements that had come in later, and IT team was very sure that the revised plan had been conveyed to marketing. Anyhow, there was no choice now but to bring the product to the market on the publicly announced date, and they did. However, this entailed shortcuts in user testing, insufficient time for a pilot run, and an inability to provide enough training to teams handling complaints, customer inquiries, and so on. Even the channel partners were not fully ready to handle this product. Obviously, the business and the project teams were moving in an uncoordinated way. Owing to this lack of alignment between Business and Technology through the development phase, the company faced a lot of turbulence in the early days. It took them a great deal of effort and cost to stabilize the product, and they probably lost some credibility in the market. Evidently, an unwavering tactical alliance that always keeps Business and Technology on the same page on market commitments has no substitute, particularly in this digital era.*

---

## About the BITA Calculator

The BITA calculator is a simple assessment tool for estimating your BITA score. It consists of a list of statements, each of which can be responded with a Y if true, else left blank. These statements are designed to estimate your scores with respect to the seven dimensions of BITA and calculate your overall BITA Index. The statements are scattered, i.e., not bunched into dimensions, to avoid extempore responses. Each statement tests your alignment to a dimension, though some statements may map to more than one dimension. It is a first attempt at creating a measuring tool of this kind, and I do concede that there is room for making it more situational, precise, and entertaining. (Updates can be downloaded from www.alignedtowin.com) The tool is intended to mark your bearings on your BITA journey and set you in the right direction toward your goal. You can, of course, modify the tool by inserting more statements, deleting or editing some statements, and creating different versions, as you advance on your journey. You can also set your own benchmarks on what constitutes a low or a high score and use these for tracking trends over time.

## Method

1. Appoint a tool administrator (TA).
2. The TA will load the statements on an excel file and distribute this among selected respondents.
3. If number of respondents is few (<5), photocopied paper questionnaire can also be used.
4. You can also download the excel version of the tool from *Aligned-ToWin.Com*
5. The TA will guide the respondents as necessary in completing the feedback.
6. The respondents respond with clear *Y* (yes) or *blank* (no) to each statement and submit this back to the TA.
7. For each Y, the TA will enter a 1 in the respondent's *score sheet* against the statement number, *under the appropriate dimension* using the *check sheet* (scoring guide) for reference. (Figure 6.2)
8. Finally, the TA will add up the 1s under each dimension and compute the dimension-wise and overall BITA score *for each respondent.*
9. The composite score of multiple respondents is the *average* of all responses against each dimension. It is a good practice to report scores for Business, IT, and Enterprise level separately.

As we go through this chapter, this process will be further crystallized. For best results, I suggest you run the test with senior members of both Business and Technology organizations. Initially, this exercise is recommended to be conducted bi-yearly, and once your benchmark index is reached, you may reduce the frequency to once a year. The set of participants may be different in each run.

For tabulating the score, take a blank *score sheet* (provided in this chapter) for each respondent and keep it alongside the *check sheet* (which is also provided). The *check sheet* is a reference table, which is the key to map a statement to a dimension. The check sheet is *not* shown to the respondents and is available with the TA only. For each statement that is responded with a Y, the scorer (typically the TA) puts a 1 in the score sheet *under the corresponding dimension*. If the response is *not* Y, nothing is scored for that statement. In the *example* shown in Figure 6.2, the response is Y against statements 2 and 3. According to the check sheet, these statements correspond to intellect and strategy dimensions, respectively. A "1" (one) is thus entered in the relevant rows/columns of the score sheet, as shown. This is helpful as an illustration, but oversimplistic.

| St. no | Statement | | Response |
|---|---|---|---|
| 1 | Statement one | | |
| 2 | Statement two | *Statement list* | Y |
| 3 | Statement three | | Y |
| 4 | Statement four | | |

| CHECK Sheet | | | | | | | |
|---|---|---|---|---|---|---|---|
| Statement number | Culture | Strategy | Structure | Process | Intellect | Function | Tactics |
| 1 | 1 | | | | | | |
| 2 | | | | | 1 | | |
| 3 | | 1 | | | | | |
| 4 | | | | 1 | | 1 | |

| SCORE Sheet | | | | | | | |
|---|---|---|---|---|---|---|---|
| Statement number | Culture | Strategy | Structure | Process | Intellect | Function | Tactics |
| 1 | | | | | | | |
| 2 | | | | | 1 | | |
| 3 | | 1 | | | | | |
| 4 | | | | | | | |

*Figure 6.2  BITA scoring process*

We will look at a more realistic BITA computation later in this chapter. We contended earlier that Business and IT must think, build, and operate *together* for real and sustained alignment that leads to long-term business value. Accordingly, we have split the statements into three sets, clustered under the Think, Build, and Operate (TBO) headings, though this is optional. Your responses to these statements will therefore also enable you to ascertain if you need to ramp up your efforts on any of the TBO axes.

It is recommended to get the CIO, solution architects, IT delivery and operations managers, chief marketing officer (CMO), product manager, customer service head, and account managers on-boarded for this. You may like to have a *dedicated workshop* on BITA with the group of chosen participants, and as part of this workshop, this tool can be run to determine your BITA index. As a progressive enterprise, the modality of conducting the assessment is a matter of your preference. Organizations that have a clear view of where they stand on their BITA journey have a far better chance of succeeding in their digital mission.

Let us get started. Keep about 30 minutes for completing each of the three lists (T, B, O). Use the first response that comes to your mind after you read the statement. Do not pause to reflect or overthink. I have found that instinctive responses generally lead to more accurate results.

Some statements are *designed* to be subjective so that individual *opinions* from folks at different levels may be factored in the BITA score. It is important that the respondents are reasonably familiar with the company's Business and Technology landscape. In an organization that is aspiring to lead in the digital economy, *all* the team members of both Business and Technology organizations should have at least a general awareness of their shared beliefs, strategy, tactics, and so on, on which the statements are based. Thus, if you happen to be *not* sure of the truth of a statement, you are advised to respond with *N* (or blank). For example, you are *expected* to know—whether you are from Business or IT organization—if the company's "Long-term business strategy is the basis of IT roadmap and architecture." If you do not have a clue about this, then consider N (blank) for this statement. Even if at some level this statement is true, from *your* perspective it is not. But most statements, hopefully, will not cause such dilemmas.

The list is by no means a comprehensive one for each dimension. For example, the statements mapping to *tactics* should not be taken to be a complete list of *all* that is required for tactical alignment. However, it should point you to the dimensions that you need to prioritize to improve your overall BITA index. In more advanced versions, the statements may be tailored as per the organization's maturity, assigned weights according to its needs and priorities, and have graded responses on say, a 1–5 scale rather than a simple 1 or 0.

Some of the statements may appear complex, especially if you are from an organization where Business and Technology do interwork but are not strongly aligned. This is by design, as BITA is also about Business and Technology having an in-depth understanding of issues affecting themselves and each other. Further, not everyone using the tool is expected to be at the same level, which necessitates a heterogeneous mix.

Note: A few times you will come across statements like, *"As a Business (IT) person, I understand the IT (Business) organization structure." This implies if you are a Business person you understand the IT organization structure, or vice versa.*

---

**List 1: Think:** *Plan*—Strategy, Roadmap | *Design*—Innovation, Improvement | *Share*—Knowledge, Ideas, Culture | *Measure*—Trends, Analysis

---

*Table 6.1 Think*

| S.No | Statement | Response |
|------|-----------|----------|
| 1 | I have participated in a belief session conducted by our top management at least once in the last year. | |
| 2 | IT in our organization is not just a support arm for technical services, but also advises Business on technology trends and practices. | |
| 3 | We have a clearly articulated mission, frequently reinforced by the top management, that envisages the use of digital technologies as a vehicle for enterprise growth. | |
| 4 | Business outcomes (like time-to-market, effectiveness of digital campaigns) are a measure of IT success in our company | |

*Table 6.1 Think*

| S.No | Statement | Response |
|------|-----------|----------|
| 5 | We have a supportive IT foundation on which the future business services can be built quickly and efficiently. That is, our IT architecture is not an obstacle to our future growth. | |
| 6 | If I have a great technical idea, I feel encouraged to walk up to the CTO/CIO or CMO to discuss it. | |
| 7 | We have regular Business–IT interlocks to assure that our IT processes and systems are tuned to the ever-evolving needs of the business. | |
| 8 | One of our strengths is our business savvy IT folks, most of whom understand the competitive landscape, regulations, customer expectations, etc. | |
| 9 | One of our strengths is our technology-savvy business folks, most of whom are familiar with concepts like Internet Protocol (IP), IT architecture, Cloud, Big data, etc. | |
| 10 | Sensing from the present momentum, I feel quite confident that we will meet our digital transformation objectives, in the next one year. (This is my opinion.) | |
| 11 | I feel empowered because I know exactly how my work is contributing to my company's business. | |
| 12 | Business and IT often have joint brain-storming sessions to arrive at make or buy decisions, driven by time-to-market or cost considerations. | |
| 13 | We have many success stories of Business and IT achieving together (winning business, solving customer problems) that I believe could be used to attract exceptional talent in our company. | |
| 14 | I can recall at least one offsite event (office get-together, outing, social function) in the last one year in which both Business and IT folks took part (not just the CIO and CMO but larger group). | |
| 15 | I have gone through our IT strategy. It is well aligned with the Business strategy. It won't be wrong to say that our IT's mission is to make the business successful. | |
| 16 | I have been part of (or aware of) a meeting where Business and IT shared and debated their strategy/roadmap with each other with a view to align. | |
| 17 | Our competitive landscape, offerings portfolio, customer expectations, and strategy is explained to IT during induction of employees (or through subsequent programs) by Business. | |

*Table 6.1 Think*

| S.No | Statement | Response |
|------|-----------|----------|
| 18 | We understand that the market is dynamic. Hence, we reassess IT skills yearly on both Technology and Business attributes, if necessary, through an external consultant. | |
| 19 | In my experience, I have found that senior business leaders in our company directly interact with our tech specialists on business/customer issues. We do not follow a hierarchy-driven protocol. | |
| 20 | As a Business (IT) person I have participated in at least one IT (Business) training program as a student or instructor in the last six months. | |
| 21 | We engage with diverse stakeholders, including partners, suppliers, and customers for their inputs in charting our business/IT roadmap. | |
| 22 | Our technology capabilities, architecture, and roadmap is explained to Business during employee induction or in successive programs by IT. | |
| 23 | We periodically benchmark our IT operations performance with the industry leaders and reset our targets to meet or exceed these. | |
| 24 | We have an empowered technology council for evaluating new ideas relating to products, services, and campaigns , which consists of nominated persons from both Business and IT. | |
| 25 | One of the reasons I am happy to be in this company is the opportunities offered for skill building in new technology domains. | |
| 26 | I attended at least one training program on new business or technology trends in the last six months. | |
| 27 | Initiatives toward learning and adoption of new technology, like participation in development programs, matter in my performance appraisal. | |
| 28 | Selection of a technology partner for products, services, or consulting involves acceptance of both Business and IT teams in our company. | |
| 29 | I was in a product or technology training program in the last six months where both business and IT folks participated. | |
| 30 | In our last company Rewards and Recognition (R&R) event, there was at least one award given for an innovative idea around the use of new technology. | |

### Table 6.1 Think

| S.No | Statement | Response |
|------|-----------|----------|
| 31 | I am encouraged by my company to participate in industry events and seminars on technology trends. I have attended at least one in the last six months. | |
| 32 | Rotations across Business and IT functions through internal job postings are encouraged. I know of at least three such cases. | |
| 33 | The motivation and push for investing in new technology in our company often comes from the business team. | |
| 34 | I am aware of the company's overall business strategy and can trace my performance objectives and KRAs to it. | |
| 35 | Enterprise Architecture (EA), eTOM, TOGAF, etc. are some standard frameworks that aid Business–IT alignment. My organization has adopted standard frameworks in its IT architecture. | |
| 36 | I have participated in discussions between Business and IT for finalizing the high-level design of products or customizations. | |
| 37 | The speed and precision with which our IT can translate new concepts into revenue-generating products and services is an undisputed competitive advantage for our company. I can cite examples. | |
| 38 | There is an annual Internal Customer Satisfaction Survey conducted in our company to assess improvement areas. | |
| 39 | In our company, no project or investment plan is final until both Business and IT have agreed upon it. | |
| 40 | We have seasoned Technical Architects in our organization to help the Business identify, design, and build custom solutions based on emerging technologies. | |
| 41 | Over 50% of our IT investment in the year is for developing or supporting business transformation (new offerings, differentiation, digital enablement - Social, Mobility, Analytics, and Cloud [SMAC]). | |
| 42 | Apart from being IT experts, several of our IT people bring in good knowledge of our industry domain and are engaged by Business as thought leaders and strategic advisors. | |
| 43 | In the course of routine Business–IT review meetings, it is normal for IT to report on cost savings achieved through various initiatives (like reuse). | |

> **List 2: Build:** *Collaborate*—Governance, Teamwork | *Construct*—Process, Organization | *Deliver*—Projects, Solutions | *Deploy*—Technology, Best practices | *Optimize*—Time, Cost, Quality

## Table 6.2 Build

| S.No. | Statement | Response |
|---|---|---|
| 44 | I (or anyone I know) do not feel micromanaged or controlled by the supervisor. | |
| 45 | In our company, we are free to take customer problems to management without fear, and express dissent with management on issues impacting our customers. | |
| 46 | Business and IT celebrate their wins together in our company. | |
| 47 | As a Business (IT) person, I understand the IT (Business) organization. I can explain it to a customer if needed. | |
| 48 | We have Business Analysts (or equivalent) in our company as the single-point interface between Business and IT. | |
| 49 | My performance goals and KRAs are dependent on the Business achieving its mission. That is, if the Business fails, I fail, irrespective of whether I am from the Business or IT team. | |
| 50 | Outcome-based IT is a well-entrenched concept in my organization. For example, "Boosting customer engagement via Digital Channels" could equally be a goal for IT as well as Business. | |
| 51 | The decision to bid for a contract is made jointly by Business and IT (except in case of "standard" offers). | |
| 52 | Our IT strategy and status are part of the agenda of our company's seniormost leadership team meetings. | |
| 53 | We have systems to identify unexpected gaps between Business and IT strategies due to market dynamics and make timely course corrections. | |
| 54 | We hold a customer meet at least once a year with our key customers and partners, which is attended by leaders from both Business and IT. | |
| 55 | The processes in our organization, at least those that I am familiar with, are designed to make it easy for people to get things done. | |
| 56 | IT team members routinely participate in sales/marketing conferences in our company. | |

**Table 6.2 Build**

| S.No. | Statement | Response |
|---|---|---|
| 57 | We are able to respond quickly to business needs because our process workflow, particularly for IT requests, is designed to be fast and quick, with minimum approvals. | |
| 58 | Business teams share the updated plans and progress with designated members of the IT team (e.g., BA) every month in our organization. | |
| 59 | Our IT organization is quick to align its skills and structure with the changing needs of the business. | |
| 60 | I believe that our IT is spending more time and money on "Change the Business" (transformation and new initiatives) than on "Run the Business" (routine operations, upkeep, keeping the light bulbs on). | |
| 61 | We have launched products or services in the market based on at least one of these—Internet of Things (IoT), Cloud, Mobility (apps), Big Data. | |
| 62 | Our IT processes are well documented and available on a public folder (or intranet), accessible to both Business and IT. | |
| 63 | For some IT/Technology positions, it is common in our company for business leaders to interview (IT) candidates. | |
| 64 | We have a new product introduction process clearly outlined which requires Business and IT to work together on a new market offering from its inception to launch. | |
| 65 | Our marketing campaign relies on customer data managed by IT. A formal process exists for Business and IT to jointly assure the integrity of customer data. | |
| 66 | Our change management process for delivering IT products and customizations (change requests) is agreed with Business. | |
| 67 | The User Acceptance Testing of IT deliverables is conducted exclusively by the Business (without IT intervention). | |
| 68 | I count our ability to launch new business services on time as one of our organizational strengths. | |
| 69 | Our IT development follows the iterative (agile) model to incorporate changing business requirements without hampering our time-to-market for new offerings. | |
| 70 | Business and Technology teams meet frequently and regularly (say every week) specifically to discuss pending and escalated customer issues. | |
| 71 | Business and IT together review (steer) critical or transformational IT projects through senior-level involvement (governance). | |

*Table 6.2 Build*

| S.No. | Statement | Response |
|-------|-----------|----------|
| 72 | In our company customer needs drive the proactive adoption of new trends like ecommerce platform, cloud-based offerings, BDA, etc. I can cite examples. | |
| 73 | Finalizing the specifications and design for new IT development is accomplished collaboratively with inputs and agreement from both Business and IT. | |
| 74 | We lay strong emphasis on information security. However, our security stance is not an impediment to smooth business conduct. | |
| 75 | Business and IT commonly work together in preparing the response to a Request for Proposal (RFP). | |
| 76 | We have invested in tools to gauge our customers' sentiments through social media and use this to calibrate our response to customers. | |

**List-3: Operate:** *Execute*—Sell, Service, Install | *Monitor*—Process, Performance, Cost | *Control*—Assets, Policies | *Support*—Customer experience, enterprise productivity, data privacy, and security

*Table 6.3 Operate*

| S.No | Statement | Response |
|------|-----------|----------|
| 77 | We promote and encourage BYOD in our organization. | |
| 78 | The quality of the business outcome (like customer experience, revenue growth, speed-to-market) is a measure of IT performance too in our company. | |
| 79 | More often than not, I talk to the person who sits on the same floor as me, than send them an e-mail. | |
| 80 | If my business card described me as a Customer Satisfier instead of my present title, it would do full justice to my role. By customer here, I mean the end, or external, customer. | |
| 81 | Our ability to offer personalized customer solutions based on the use of advanced technologies like Big data is an undisputed success factor for the company. | |
| 82 | Business and IT regularly review the customer service data (like response time to complaints, escalated problems) as a reliable indicator of customer's overall perception about us. | |

*Table 6.3 Operate*

| S.No | Statement | Response |
|------|-----------|----------|
| 83 | Business and technology teams routinely participate together in meetings with technology partners/vendors in our company. | |
| 84 | The Business owns the IT budget as it has a direct impact on the P&L. Therefore, Business and IT jointly decide on business case for IT expenditure. | |
| 85 | Business and IT are jointly engaged in innovation and transformation in methods of doing business, e.g., proposals, offers, campaigns, bills and receipts, upsells. | |
| 86 | Participation of the relevant team members from the IT organization in business conferences is a routine matter in our company. | |
| 87 | Our IT team members often visit our dealers/field-offices to assess the market pulse and experiences of local staff in working with our IT systems. | |
| 88 | We track Business Value of IT focusing on business outcomes influenced by IT (like Customer Experience, Revenue/Upsells, Cost-Savings). | |
| 89 | Business and IT periodically meet to discuss the feasibility of current IT services—e.g., applications that can be retired, merged, consolidated, enhanced, or upgraded. | |
| 90 | My company has the IT tools and expertise to gather and act upon market intelligence and voice-of-customer in a consistent and timely manner. | |
| 91 | I am part of, or am aware of, the regular forums in which expenditure on IT infrastructure and services (capex and opex) is reported by IT to Business. | |
| 92 | I have the right tools, connectivity, and devices to access the data I require for making decisions that impact my internal and external customers. | |
| 93 | A mechanism exists in our company to get customer feedback on quality of our service/product and use this to improve the quality. | |
| 94 | IT in our company is not considered too "narrow" or "maintenance-centric" to influence business. | |
| 95 | As a Business (IT) person, I know exactly whom to go to if I have an IT (Business) problem. | |
| 96 | Our IT systems undergo annual refresh cycles and system upgrades and capacity dimensioning in consultation with Business to keep pace with the changing business requirements. | |
| 97 | We have regular (scheduled) forums for presentation by IT to Business on customer operations and delivery performance and trends. | |

*Table 6.3 Operate*

| S.No | Statement | Response |
|------|-----------|----------|
| 98 | In our company, both Business and IT are in the front-end delivering customer proposals, solutions, service. IT is not a backend function. | |
| 99 | We do not launch a new product or service until we have built the capability in IT to fully support it in the market. | |
| 100 | Once Business and IT have agreed on a plan, I would not hesitate to announce it publicly, including to customers. I have confidence in IT's ability to deliver on their promise. | |
| 101 | At least once in six months, IT updates business on the capacity of the IT infrastructure (like servers, storage, bandwidth) to support business needs and decide jointly on next steps. | |
| 102 | We have an agreed business continuity plan to keep our essential services working in the event of a calamity that shuts down our core IT systems. | |
| 103 | Customers and business folks can access our customer complaints tracking tool without IT intervention. | |
| 104 | After the resolution of severe customer complaints, IT team provides a root cause analysis report to Business team. | |
| 105 | Our Change Management Process sets clear roles and responsibilities for Business and IT in various stages of the delivery cycle. I understand the process clearly. | |

*Table 6.4 Score sheet List-1 [Think]*

| Statement Number | Culture | Strategy | Structure | Process | Intellect | Function | Tactics |
|------------------|---------|----------|-----------|---------|-----------|----------|---------|
| 1 | | | | | | | |
| 2 | | | | | | | |
| 3 | | | | | | | |
| 4 | | | | | | | |
| 5 | | | | | | | |
| 6 | | | | | | | |
| 7 | | | | | | | |
| 8 | | | | | | | |
| 9 | | | | | | | |
| 10 | | | | | | | |
| 11 | | | | | | | |
| 12 | | | | | | | |

*Table 6.4 Score sheet List-1 [Think]*

| Statement Number | Culture | Strategy | Structure | Process | Intellect | Function | Tactics |
|---|---|---|---|---|---|---|---|
| 13 | | | | | | | |
| 14 | | | | | | | |
| 15 | | | | | | | |
| 16 | | | | | | | |
| 17 | | | | | | | |
| 18 | | | | | | | |
| 19 | | | | | | | |
| 20 | | | | | | | |
| 21 | | | | | | | |
| 22 | | | | | | | |
| 23 | | | | | | | |
| 24 | | | | | | | |
| 25 | | | | | | | |
| 26 | | | | | | | |
| 27 | | | | | | | |
| 28 | | | | | | | |
| 29 | | | | | | | |
| 30 | | | | | | | |
| 31 | | | | | | | |
| 32 | | | | | | | |
| 33 | | | | | | | |
| 34 | | | | | | | |
| 35 | | | | | | | |
| 36 | | | | | | | |
| 37 | | | | | | | |
| 38 | | | | | | | |
| 39 | | | | | | | |
| 40 | | | | | | | |
| 41 | | | | | | | |
| 42 | | | | | | | |
| 43 | | | | | | | |
| TOTAL | | | | | | | |

## Table 6.5 Score sheet List-2 [Build]

| Statement Number | Culture | Strategy | Structure | Process | Intellect | Function | Tactics |
|---|---|---|---|---|---|---|---|
| 44 | | | | | | | |
| 45 | | | | | | | |
| 46 | | | | | | | |
| 47 | | | | | | | |
| 48 | | | | | | | |
| 49 | | | | | | | |
| 50 | | | | | | | |
| 51 | | | | | | | |
| 52 | | | | | | | |
| 53 | | | | | | | |
| 54 | | | | | | | |
| 55 | | | | | | | |
| 56 | | | | | | | |
| 57 | | | | | | | |
| 58 | | | | | | | |
| 59 | | | | | | | |
| 60 | | | | | | | |
| 61 | | | | | | | |
| 62 | | | | | | | |
| 63 | | | | | | | |
| 64 | | | | | | | |
| 65 | | | | | | | |
| 66 | | | | | | | |
| 67 | | | | | | | |
| 68 | | | | | | | |
| 69 | | | | | | | |
| 70 | | | | | | | |
| 71 | | | | | | | |
| 72 | | | | | | | |
| 73 | | | | | | | |
| 74 | | | | | | | |
| 75 | | | | | | | |
| 76 | | | | | | | |
| TOTAL | | | | | | | |

*Table 6.6 Score Sheet List 3 [Operate]*

| Statement Number | Cul-ture | Strategy | Structure | Pro-cess | Intellect | Function | Tactics |
|---|---|---|---|---|---|---|---|
| 77 | | | | | | | |
| 78 | | | | | | | |
| 79 | | | | | | | |
| 80 | | | | | | | |
| 81 | | | | | | | |
| 82 | | | | | | | |
| 83 | | | | | | | |
| 84 | | | | | | | |
| 85 | | | | | | | |
| 86 | | | | | | | |
| 87 | | | | | | | |
| 88 | | | | | | | |
| 89 | | | | | | | |
| 90 | | | | | | | |
| 91 | | | | | | | |
| 92 | | | | | | | |
| 93 | | | | | | | |
| 94 | | | | | | | |
| 95 | | | | | | | |
| 96 | | | | | | | |
| 97 | | | | | | | |
| 98 | | | | | | | |
| 99 | | | | | | | |
| 100 | | | | | | | |
| 101 | | | | | | | |
| 102 | | | | | | | |
| 103 | | | | | | | |
| 104 | | | | | | | |
| 105 | | | | | | | |
| TOTAL | | | | | | | |

| | Culture | Strategy | Structure | Process | Intellect | Function | Tactics |
|---|---|---|---|---|---|---|---|
| GRAND TOTAL | | | | | | | |

*Table 6.7 Check sheet*

| THINK | | | | | | | | BUILD | | | | | | | | OPERATE | | | | | | | |
|---|---|---|---|---|---|---|---|---|---|---|---|---|---|---|---|---|---|---|---|---|---|---|---|
| St | C | Sy | Se | P | I | F | T | St | C | Sy | Se | P | I | F | T | St | C | Sy | Se | P | I | F | T |
| 1 | 1 |  |  |  |  |  |  | 44 | 1 |  |  |  |  |  |  | 77 | 1 |  |  |  | 1 | 1 | 1 |  |
| 2 |  | 1 |  |  | 1 |  |  | 45 | 1 |  |  |  |  |  |  | 78 |  |  |  | 1 | 1 |  | 1 |  |
| 3 |  | 1 |  |  |  |  |  | 46 | 1 |  |  |  |  |  |  | 79 | 1 |  |  |  |  |  |  | 1 |
| 4 |  |  |  | 1 |  | 1 |  | 47 |  |  | 1 |  |  |  |  | 80 | 1 |  |  | 1 |  |  |  | 1 |
| 5 |  | 1 |  |  |  |  |  | 48 |  |  | 1 |  |  |  |  | 81 |  |  |  |  |  |  |  | 1 |
| 6 | 1 |  |  |  |  |  |  | 49 | 1 | 1 |  |  |  |  |  | 82 |  |  |  |  |  |  | 1 | 1 |
| 7 |  |  |  |  | 1 |  |  | 50 |  | 1 |  |  |  |  |  | 83 |  |  |  |  |  |  |  | 1 |
| 8 |  |  | 1 |  |  |  |  | 51 |  |  |  |  |  | 1 |  | 84 |  |  |  |  |  | 1 |  |  |
| 9 |  |  | 1 |  | 1 |  |  | 52 |  | 1 |  |  | 1 |  |  | 85 |  |  |  |  |  |  |  | 1 |
| 10 |  | 1 |  |  |  |  |  | 53 |  | 1 |  |  |  |  |  | 86 |  |  | 1 |  |  |  |  |  |
| 11 | 1 |  |  |  |  |  |  | 54 |  |  |  |  |  |  |  | 87 |  |  |  |  |  |  |  | 1 |
| 12 |  | 1 |  |  |  |  |  | 55 |  |  |  | 1 |  |  |  | 88 |  |  |  |  |  |  | 1 |  |
| 13 | 1 |  |  |  |  | 1 |  | 56 | 1 |  |  |  |  |  |  | 89 |  |  |  |  |  |  | 1 | 1 |
| 14 | 1 |  |  |  |  | 1 |  | 57 |  |  |  | 1 |  | 1 |  | 90 |  |  |  |  |  |  | 1 | 1 |
| 15 |  | 1 |  |  |  |  |  | 58 |  | 1 |  |  |  |  |  | 91 |  |  |  |  | 1 |  |  |  |
| 16 |  | 1 |  |  |  | 1 |  | 59 |  |  | 1 |  |  | 1 |  | 92 |  |  |  |  |  |  |  | 1 |
| 17 |  |  | 1 |  | 1 |  |  | 60 |  |  |  |  |  | 1 |  | 93 |  |  |  |  |  |  |  | 1 |

*Table 6.7 Check sheet*

### THINK

| St | C | Sy | Se | P | I | F | T |
|----|---|----|----|---|---|---|---|
| 18 | 1 |    | 1  |   |   |   |   |
| 19 | 1 |    | 1  |   |   |   |   |
| 20 |   | 1  |    |   |   |   |   |
| 21 |   |    | 1  |   | 1 |   |   |
| 22 |   | 1  |    |   |   |   |   |
| 23 |   |    |    |   |   |   | 1 |
| 24 |   |    |    |   | 1 |   |   |
| 25 |   |    | 1  |   | 1 |   |   |
| 26 | 1 |    |    |   | 1 |   |   |
| 27 | 1 |    |    |   |   |   |   |
| 28 |   |    |    |   |   | 1 | 1 |
| 29 |   |    | 1  |   | 1 |   |   |
| 30 | 1 |    |    |   | 1 |   |   |
| 31 |   |    |    |   | 1 |   |   |
| 32 | 1 |    | 1  |   |   |   |   |
| 33 | 1 |    |    |   | 1 |   |   |
| 34 |   | 1  |    |   |   |   |   |

### BUILD

| St | C | Sy | Se | P | I | F | T |
|----|---|----|----|---|---|---|---|
| 61 |   |    |    |   | 1 |   | 1 |
| 62 |   |    |    | 1 |   |   |   |
| 63 | 1 |    | 1  |   |   |   |   |
| 64 |   |    |    | 1 | 1 |   |   |
| 65 |   |    |    |   | 1 | 1 |   |
| 66 |   |    |    | 1 |   |   |   |
| 67 |   |    |    | 1 |   |   | 1 |
| 68 |   |    |    | 1 |   |   |   |
| 69 |   |    |    | 1 |   |   |   |
| 70 |   |    |    |   |   |   | 1 |
| 71 |   |    |    |   |   | 1 |   |
| 72 |   |    |    |   | 1 |   |   |
| 73 |   |    |    | 1 |   |   | 1 |
| 74 |   |    |    | 1 |   |   | 1 |
| 75 |   |    |    |   |   | 1 | 1 |
| 76 |   |    |    | 1 |   |   | 1 |

### OPERATE

| St  | C  | Sy | Se | P  | I  | F  | T  |
|-----|----|----|----|----|----|----|----|
| 94  |    |    |    |    |    | 1  |    |
| 95  |    |    | 1  |    |    |    | 1  |
| 96  |    |    |    | 1  |    |    | 1  |
| 97  |    |    |    | 1  |    |    | 1  |
| 98  |    |    | 1  |    | 1  |    |    |
| 99  |    |    |    |    |    |    | 1  |
| 100 |    | 1  |    |    |    |    | 1  |
| 101 |    |    |    |    |    |    | 1  |
| 102 |    |    |    | 1  |    |    | 1  |
| 103 |    |    |    | 1  |    |    | 1  |
| 104 |    |    |    | 1  | 1  |    | 1  |
| 105 |    |    |    |    |    |    | 1  |
| Tot | 22 | 18 | 18 | 25 | 22 | 24 | 29 |

*Table 6.7 Check sheet*

| | THINK | | | | | | | | BUILD | | | | | | | | OPERATE | | | | | | | |
|---|---|---|---|---|---|---|---|---|---|---|---|---|---|---|---|---|---|---|---|---|---|---|---|---|
| St | C | Sy | Se | P | I | F | T | St | C | Sy | Se | P | I | F | T | St | C | Sy | Se | P | I | F | T |
| 35 | | | | 1 | 1 | | | | | | | | | | | | | | | | | | | |
| 36 | | | | 1 | | | | | | | | | | | | | | | | | | | | |
| 37 | | 1 | | | | 1 | | | | | | | | | | | | | | | | | | |
| 38 | 1 | | | 1 | | | | | | | | | | | | | | | | | | | | |
| 39 | | 1 | | 1 | | | | | | | | | | | | | | | | | | | | |
| 40 | | | 1 | | | | | | | | | | | | | | | | | | | | | |
| 41 | | 1 | | | 1 | | | | | | | | | | | | | | | | | | | |
| 42 | | | 1 | 1 | | | | | | | | | | | | | | | | | | | | |
| 43 | | | | | | 1 | | | | | | | | | | | | | | | | | | |

*Table 6.8 BITA scoring example*

| | | Cul-ture | Strat-egy | Struc-ture | Pro-cess | Intel-lect | Func-tion | Tact-ics | BITA |
|---|---|---|---|---|---|---|---|---|---|
| | | **Example** | | | | | | | |
| | | **BUSINESS or IT or OVERALL** | | | | | | | |
| | <Name> | Cul-ture | Strat-egy | Struc-ture | Pro-cess | Intel-lect | Func-tion | Tact-ics | BITA |
| A | Max Y-count (Fixed-do not change) | 22 | 18 | 18 | 25 | 22 | 24 | 29 | 158 |
| B | Raw Y-Count (Actual Count) | 12 | 8 | 10 | 6 | 8 | 5 | 8 | 57 |
| C | Score ((B/A)*100 | 55 | 44 | 56 | 24 | 36 | 21 | 28 | **37.6** |

The total scores may be entered as shown in Table 6.8. The actual count of 1s in each dimension is entered in row B. In the case of multiple respondents, the average score for each dimension is entered in Row B. Row A, which is *fixed*, shows the *max* possible count, that is, the total number of statements corresponding to that dimension out of the full set. You may note that the total number of statements is 105, but the total of Row A is 158. This is because some of the statements correspond to *two* dimensions.

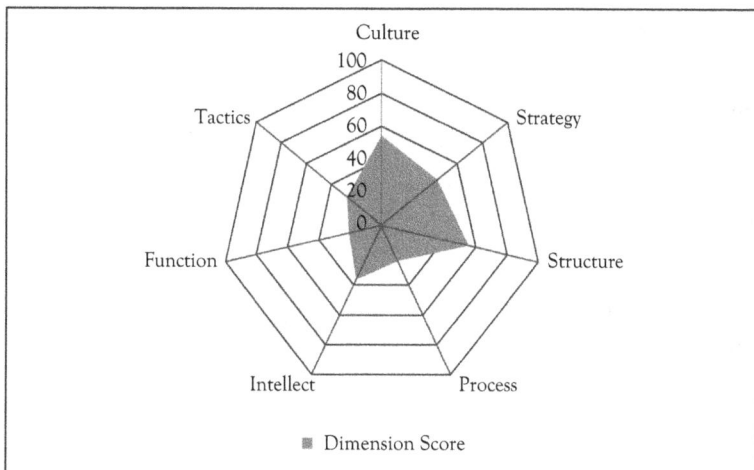

*Figure 6.3 BITA score chart*

The score for each dimension is calculated on a base of 100 by simply taking the ratio of Actual (row B) and Maximum (row A) count and multiplying by 100.

Plotting the final scores (row C) on a radar graph as in Figure 6.3 gives an excellent relational view of the scores on each dimension. The graph tells us here that while the organization has relatively good cultural and structural alignment, it needs to pull up its alignment score on other dimensions. In the book *Mastering the 7 Dimensions of Business-Technology Alignment*[1] by the same author, a few approaches to improve the dimensional scores are discussed in detail with exercises and examples. As we said earlier, all dimensions are connected. For example, if you align strongly on your strategy, without strengthening the capacity to execute it (tactical alignment), it wouldn't take you very far. Or, if you align on strategy and tactics dimensions but lack the structure (people, competencies) and process alignment required to deliver, the desired outcomes will elude you.

## What's a Good BITA Score?

If you are expecting a centum score on BITA—or even any of its dimensions—you are setting yourself up for disappointment. Let's face it. There are far too many variables in every dimension of BITA for any one enterprise to achieve perfection in the initial attempt, though it is a theoretical possibility.

There are no benchmarks yet available for the BITA scores. Hence, I am relying on my own assessment, which is based on the scores of enterprises at different stages of BITA. When I performed the test for an organization, which I rate the highest in BITA among the few organizations that I assessed, I achieved average scores of 45–60 on each dimension and an overall BITA of 55. Does this mean this is the most one can aspire to? Probably not. It is certainly rewarding to aim higher, and more importantly, to *grow* from wherever you may be right now. For this reason, I may put an organization which has moved from, say, 25–40 a bit higher than the organization that is stagnating at 42 in the same period.

On the other hand, another company that I conducted this test for surprisingly scored as low as 7–10 on culture, strategy, process, intellect,

*Table 6.9 BITA score ranges*

| SN | BITA Level—where are you on your BITA journey | Score range (Overall BITA) | Semesterly improvement target | Retest in |
|---|---|---|---|---|
| 1 | Excellent—Well settled | 80+ | Maintain | 1 year |
| 2 | Very Good—Arrived | 60–80 | 10% | 1 year |
| 3 | Good—Almost there | 50–60 | 20% | 6–9 months |
| 4 | Fair—On the right track | 40–50 | 25% | 6 months |
| 5 | Deficient—Need course correction | 30–40 | 25% | 3 months |
| 6 | Low—Lack momentum | 20–30 | 35% | 3 months |
| 7 | Nonexistent—Not started | <20 | 50% | 2 months |

and function alignment while it scored 20 on tactical alignment. Overall, it was at about 11. Having some knowledge of where this company is in its thought process and actions regarding BITA, I think this should form the lower end of the BITA scale. Anything lower would indeed make it rather uphill to achieve a respectable score.

Going by these experiments, companies with an overall BITA score of over 50 in their first assessment should feel reasonably good about their prospects in the digital economy. Taking this further, the progressive score ranges and the *targeted* semesterly improvement in the scores would be as per Table 6.9.

It would be helpful to further plot a line graph over time for each dimension (and the overall BITA score) to monitor the trends. Any dimension showing a *downward* movement should instantly ring an alert and must become the focus of immediate correction.

Variants are possible, which may perhaps yield more accurate results. One such could be to rate each statement on a scale of 0 to 4 (Never Demonstrated → Major Strength) instead of just 0 or 1 and calculate the scores accordingly. This will enable monitoring the improvement at the level of each *statement.* There is indeed enormous scope for innovating as we go to make this tool a very precise indicator of BITA in your organization.

# CHAPTER 7

# Setting the Stage for the Digital Enterprise

Thus far in this book, our focus has been on the importance of Business–Technology alignment in the digital era and its role as an enabler of success for the digital enterprise. We established that as the focus of technology has shifted to *business* outcome, one can no longer separate Business from Technology. In other words, Business and Technology are fused at the level of their culture, strategy, structure, process, intellect, function, and tactics.

Much as business management and people management have been integral to enterprise success, the new economy also requires a strong focus on *Technology Management* as a driver of growth and success. Technology Management—or managing technology for business—is a vast subject, which is quickly emerging as a coveted discipline of management study and research. Technology Management does not necessitate in-depth and intricate knowledge of technology itself but requires honing the qualities that lead to its effective use for business.

Technology now has the power to alter the business and market landscape of any industry completely. Alignment between Technology and Business in this backdrop, therefore, must be a key strategic priority for the digital enterprise. As obvious as this may seem, most businesses have not been successful in driving this alignment within their organizations, as they have relied on conventional approaches and idealistic assumptions. The truth is, people are too focused on their short-term objectives to seriously work on harmonizing their Business and Technology imperatives, which "sounds like a great thing to do, but not right now." Obviously, an approach that works on the level of *injecting Business–IT alignment (BITA) into the organization's DNA* is the solution. And this, in turn, brings us back to the seven dimensions we earlier introduced, which constitute the genetic code to program the successful digital enterprise.

Even after at least a decade that this has been a subject of discussion, most organizations cannot boast of having reached the level of alignment required to drive their continuous growth in a tough market. Successfully navigating the ocean of digital business requires a more inclusive and *rounded* approach to alignment, which focuses on *each* of the *seven* dimensions that are now familiar to us (Figure 7.1).

The term "rounded" is the key here, by which we mean that isolated focus on a set of dimensions (like strategy, process, and structure) while ignoring others is *not* going to get you to your destination safely and quickly. In the instances depicted in Figure 7.1, A is the BITA score we depicted in the example we studied in Chapter 6 (inserted here for reference only), and B and C are hypothetical illustrations of higher BITA scores. Here, while B represents a slightly *lower* BITA than C, it is a much more *rounded* achievement (i.e., comparable results along *all* dimensions), and hence preferable to C, which is a somewhat higher BITA score overall but does not stack up comparably on the intellect dimension. This lack of roundedness is the single biggest reason for organizations not achieving targeted long-term success in their digital endeavors, despite good intentions and effort. An enterprise that prides itself on, say, its strategic and functional alignment may yet rue the fact that business results are not commensurate with expectations. They'd probably take the view that this whole BITA thing is just hype. By using the BITA tool covering a good mix of Business and Technology folks in your organization, you should be able to identify such depressions and then work to smoothen them out.

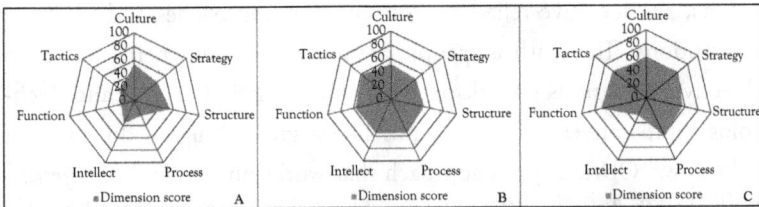

Figure 7.1 BITA score comparisons

That the digital era is upon us is unquestionable. Yet, many believe that they can brace the winds of change it brings without adjusting their sails. Their refrain is "Haven't there been environmental changes, economic upheavals, increased competition, and other barriers in the past? They couldn't slow us down. The new upstarts are the ones that need to worry." Of course, this is not an openly stated position by most companies, but deep down there is a nonchalance that this entire digital stuff is overhyped and that beyond some surface-level alterations, it is pretty much business as usual. One can only wish that they will wake up before it is too late (many are already lining up the waysides) and take some quick steps in the right direction.

On the other extreme are the new-wave digital disruptors riding on a surge of innovation, chiefly technological. They have achieved some quick successes early in the game, perhaps through some tempting promotional offers, and are therefore firmly of the view that their way is the only way. Many of them scoff at conventional business management and organizational practices as "oh so old-school." If you have entered with a long-term vision, this too is an unsustainable position. Neither can one entirely ignore digital transformation, even tacitly, nor can one bypass all established practices of business management and conduct. Clearly, a middle path must be pursued on which both these proponents may walk. Therefore, we stress the need for a *well-rounded* alignment between Business and Technology, considering all the seven dimensions as of equal significance in attaining long-term business value.

---

The environment is fast changing to adapt to the mores of the digital enterprise and a digitally enabled world. Consider as an example the upheaval in financial services on the back of the digital revolution:

1. *Quite like instant messaging surpassing SMS, digital transactions are on the verge of surpassing conventional banking methods.*
2. *The digital revolution, by making it possible to be connected anywhere and anytime, has changed the way we use banking and other financial services for purchases and bill payments.*

3. *Your smartphone can replace cash and all types of cards with mobile payment solutions, becoming your digital wallet. Mobile payment is a peer-to-peer system, which has done away with many intermediaries and is rebooting the existing set-up.*

4. *Every mobile phone is a veritable ATM with the ability to send and receive money, pay for goods and services, and transfer funds.*

5. *Electronic clearing services like NEFT-RTGS and IMPS have already overtaken traditional payment systems like cheques and bank drafts. When billions of mobile users have access to digital banking services through these means, it will completely revolutionize the economy.*

6. *Biometric authentication linked with Unique Citizen ID will enable a billion plus mobile users in India alone to have online services like validation of customer record, payments, transfers, and receipts based on a unified payment interface for various modes of transactions.*

7. *This new system will unleash a fresh wave of innovation, which will lead to the demise of many existing businesses and the birth of a whole range of new ones. Imagine the amount of data created with over a billion connected users (e.g., in India) transacting online, and how this data may enrich us as a society through advanced analytics giving insights into behavior patterns, preferences, expectations, and sentiment of various classes and communities.*

There are countless other testimonies to the fact that the world is ready for digital business, imposing a need on enterprises across industries to step up. Amid these expectations, only companies that have achieved breakthrough *technological innovation* without compromising the established *rules of business* will survive. A strong BITA is thus the foundation on which a successful digital enterprise is built.

## The Characteristics of a Digital Enterprise

An enterprise that uses digital technology as a strategic tool to gain competitive advantage is a digital enterprise. A digital enterprise follows a business model that envisages the use of digital technology to conduct its internal and external business operations. Retailing via web channels, customer self-service through online portals, web-based order booking and fulfillment, targeted digital marketing campaigns, crowdsourcing of ideas to drive innovation, enabling Bring Your Own Device (BYOD) in the workplace, and using social media analytics for managing customer experience are examples of the many characteristics of digital enterprises.

Enterprises, including digital, have their own personalities, shaped by their distinct cultures. They may differ greatly in their internal dynamics, business processes, technology deployment, and addressable markets. All digital enterprises, however, conform to the pattern of a *web-based enterprise* surrounded by an ecosystem of *technology, partners, influencers, and markets* (Figure 4.1) and exhibit some standard characteristics. With a well-rounded alignment between their Business and Technology units being vital, all digital enterprises also depend a lot on the seven BITA dimensions for success and sustainability.

When an enterprise goes digital, it is swept by a new wave that changes the way it communicates with its stakeholders, including customers, partners, and employees. The traditional methods of marketing and running operations must be seriously reevaluated. As we have already discussed, its landscape begins to be dominated by new digital technologies like cloud computing, social media, mobility, and analytics until these become an intrinsic and integral part of its value proposition. As central as technology is to its existence, however, technology is not the solitary jewel on the crest of the digital enterprise. Business acumen, economic brilliance, and common sense are as relevant in a digital enterprise as in a traditional one. This fact too underlines the importance of close alignment between Business and Technology in a world where customers are becoming increasingly tech-savvy, sometimes more so than the sales professional who is trying to strike a business deal with them.

A quick enumeration of some of the characteristics that define a digital enterprise is presented in Table 7.1. Of course, not all characteristics are necessarily displayed by any one digital enterprise, but if your organization is actively embracing many of these traits, you are well on the way to becoming a digital enterprise.

*Table 7.1 Common characteristics of a digital enterprise*

|   | Perspective | Characteristics |
|---|---|---|
| 1 | Leadership | Visibly passionate about digital vision. |
|   |   | Reinforces the digital way through constant communication: Digital is our *business*, not a *channel*. |
|   |   | Develops a comprehensive strategy around the digital vision. Ensures it is understood by all. |
|   |   | Makes data-driven decisions. |
| 2 | Organization and Culture | *Everyone* shares the company's digital identity and vision. |
|   |   | Attracts/hires/assimilates talent from other industries to nurture digital initiatives. |
|   |   | Millennials are well integrated into the org structure and cultural ethos. |
|   |   | Few layers, fast growth for achievers. Values skill over experience. |
|   |   | Demonstrates a culture of innovation through internal collaboration. |
|   |   | Skills and empowerment to manage customer experience over lifecycle. |
| 3 | Business Model | Value proposition centered on revenue streams that leverage digital technology. |
|   |   | Built around value chains constituted of ecosystem partners, who may also be competitors. |
|   |   | Embraces innovation and transformation in methods of doing business, e.g., agrregation. |
|   |   | Flexible business model and business processes. |
|   |   | Monetization using nonconventional channels, like advertising. |
| 4 | Go-to-Market | Use of digital channels (web, mobile, social) for engagement with customer through lifecycle. |
|   |   | Adoption of e-commerce (e.g., B2B) for exchange of products and services. |
|   |   | New pricing and payment models. Digital revenue streams. |
|   |   | Multiple agencies collaborate digitally to service customer need. |
|   |   | Customer engagement is at the center of go-to-market (GTM) strategy. |
| 5 | Drive for Innovation | Customer-feedback-driven technology innovation. |
|   |   | Involvement of customers in innovation and ideation. |
|   |   | Recruit, promote for the innovative bend. Recognize even tried-and-failed (dare-to-try). |

| | | |
|---|---|---|
| 6 | Sales and Marketing | Analytics-driven. Use of Big Data for segmentation/target marketing. |
| | | Automated digital marketing processes, solutions and activities (e.g., campaigns). |
| | | Adoption of digital channels to transact proposals, offers, bills, and receipts. |
| | | Use of web-based automated tracker to capture VoC at all stages of customer life cycle (CLC). |
| 7 | Customer Interface | Serving a base of informed, tech-savvy, mobile, social media (SM) empowered consumers. |
| | | Able to sense customer stimuli (e.g., to churn). |
| | | Able to handle last-minute customer requests for change with ease. |
| | | Personalized customer experience at all stages of customer lifecycle (end-to-end). |
| | | Establishment of CEM for lifecycle tracking and improvement. |
| | | Use of digital tools including social media for customer service. |
| | | Engagement with customers through online chat |
| | | 24 × 7 availability to customers for service, response to queries and assistance. |
| | | Uniform experience over multiple channels: web, chat, mobile/SMS, e-mail, person-to-person. |
| 8 | Technology/IT | Aligned with Business (BITA score of 60 or above). |
| | | Leverage new technology (Cloud, Mobile, Analytics, SM) for agility and competitiveness. |
| | | Business-aligned technology roadmap and architecture. |
| a | Big data/ Analytics | Excellence in analytics: e.g., ability to visualize data using data discovery tools. |
| | | Drills down to base of pyramid for deep insights on customer preferences. |
| | | Important data sources integrated into a single BI system to facilitate decision making. |
| | | Invests in and manages large data warehouse. Appreciates importance of data. |
| b | Cloud/ mobility | Multichannel operation using social media, mobility, cloud for internal and external business |
| | | Use of mobile data for business decision making (e.g., a bank deciding on ATM locations) ). |
| | | Web/Mobile enabled customer apps (cloud-hosted) with interface to all common devices/platforms |

*(Continued)*

*Table 7.1  Common characteristics of a digital enterprise (Continued)*

|   |   |   |
|---|---|---|
|   |   | A holistic mobile strategy—for sales, service, employee engagement. |
|   |   | Uses Mobility for customer service using real-time, in-context data. |
|   |   | Uses cloud-based systems like SFDC for sales tracking |
| c | Social Media | Uses corporate social media across the network of stakeholders. |
|   |   | Social networking and collaboration to collectively solve problems. |
|   |   | Ability to assimilate social media feeds and analyze market sentiment |
| d | Security | Manages security risks in protection of Intellectual Property (IP). |
|   |   | Manages Security Operations Center (SOC) with ability to correlate event logs for fraud detection and prevention. |
|   |   | Follows latest security protocols to mitigate risks associated with use of digital channels |
| 9 | Employee Engagement | Encourages BYOD across levels, locations. |
|   |   | Mobile access to e-mail, calendar, messaging, corporate intranet, for all employees. |
|   |   | Routine apps like leave, travel are available through mobile portal. |
|   |   | Empowered employees thru innovative use of Big data and mobility. |
| 10 | Partner Management | Digital rights and royalty management of ecosystem partners. |
|   |   | Tracking and governance of ecosystem partners through online SRM initiatives. |
|   |   | Ability to work remotely yet seamlessly and securely with partners over digital channels. |
| 11 | Internal Operations | Agile SOPs and development methodology for continuous delivery and improvement. |
|   |   | Human Resources (HR), legal, supply chain (SCM), Finance—all departments execute on digital strategy. |
|   |   | Investments in digital technology cover customer solutions *as well as* back-office operations. |

A digital enterprise is almost always characterized by the application of digital technology to an innovative concept or idea. Equating innovation to risk is the biggest impediment to the emergence of a digital enterprise, not lack of ideas or technology. There is no doubt that innovation calls for some bold initiatives, but ultimately, it is what drives the digital economy. While many enterprises have based their core businesses around this model (think Airbnb, Alibaba, Amazon, Google, Netflix, Salesforce. com, Tencent, Twitter, Uber, and hundreds more), others have used this to improve some aspect of their operations.

---

*We have been used to airline self-service kiosks at most airports for many years. They are indeed a source of great convenience for the hassled business traveler who usually reaches the terminal a few crucial minutes before the flight gate closes. A few years ago, car rental company, Hertz, took the kiosk concept a step further. Initially, they deployed self-service kiosks for customers to choose their cars, complete the paperwork, and then amble across to collect the keys and drive off. Later they took this concept even further by installing dual screen kiosks. One screen provided rental options and transactional support, while the other screen—at eye level—enabled the customer to communicate with a Hertz support rep over real-time audio and video. This resulted in closer engagement and an enhanced experience which frequently translated into loyalty.*

---

**Example 7.1**

*When I walked into the posh office of the President of a mobile-services company for a meeting last year, I was struck by a large map of the country—extending from the ceiling to the floor—on the wall facing him slightly to his left. It was not a pixelated plasma screen, but a printed map showing all the principal cities and towns. LEDs adorned each town and city on the map. Depending on whether, at the end of the last day, that town/city was below, equal (± 10 percent) or above its revenue target, the LEDs were lit red, orange, or green, being controlled by a server somewhere that sent appropriate signals based on daily status reports fed to it from sales offices. The map was liberally interspersed with green and orange dots but had a fair sprinkling of red. Guess who the president was on the call with*

*that afternoon? I was impressed by the simple yet effective medium of keep-*
*ing your finger always on the pulse of the problem—far better than reams*
*of sales reports mailed to you from all corners!*

*When I expressed my amazement, he told me that I hadn't seen any-*
*thing yet! He showed me another map—this time on the computer screen on*
*his desk—and invited me to click anywhere. When I did so, a zoomed-in*
*picture of the spot I had clicked appeared with a lot of detail. What stood*
*out was several colored spots. On clicking further, I got a better-resolved*
*image of the area. He explained that the orange, green, blue (and some red)*
*spots represented individual mobile towers in the zoomed-in locality, the*
*colors indicating their financial viability. Thus, a green tower meant that*
*traffic (and hence revenues) from that tower adequately covered the cost of*
*its operation and that it was showing profits. Blue indicated that it was*
*close to breaking even, while red meant it was a loss-making proposition.*
*Orange dots meant that the base station was running over its capacity. This*
*system enabled him to quickly decide on the redeployment of assets by mov-*
*ing loss-making base stations to augment capacity in the more profitable*
*sections of the town, without having to invest in expensive new equipment.*
*The excessive amount of backend gleaning and churning of information to*
*present complex data in such a simple and intuitive fashion is made possi-*
*ble by Big data, Cloud, mobility, and advanced analytics coming together*
*in a harmonious interplay to aid business decision making. Think about*
*how digital solutions could help you to stay agile in a competitive market.*

## The Non-Characteristics of a Digital Enterprise

In as much as we could draw out a list of some of the *desired* characteristics of a digital enterprise, we could also list down the *inhibitors* to digital evolution. Of course, not displaying the *desired* characteristics itself
would suffice to throttle your aspirations of going digital. Unfortunately,
it is not just a simple game of antonyms. There are some subtle characteristics that could water down your most ambitious plans if not recognized
and addressed early in the game. Hence while doing the opposite of the
characteristics mentioned in the previous table would undoubtedly prove
an inhibitor, especially if it is rampant across the list, some other traits
can block your path *even* if you are conforming to many of the desired

characteristics. Some of these are very commonly found even in the most enlightened companies and are worth mentioning here.

**Inertia:** Most managers are resistant to change, more so when the change is transformational, as they see the associated risks at cross-purposes with their aspirations of job security and growth. They are well ensconced in their comfort zones and resist internally induced disruptions. Many a time, good ideas are not allowed even to reach the top where decisions could be taken about their cultivation.

**Inflexibility:** Given the speed at which markets, technologies, and customer expectations are moving, a company whose leadership team sticks too long to conventional approaches is at high risk. You cannot transform your technology or business platform without first transforming your mindset and cultural backdrop.

**Bureaucracy:** Many companies still have too many hops for decision making, which inhibits the speed of response. In other words, they do not have adequately empowered customer-facing teams. This is where companies that are turning digital lose out to digital start-ups (born-digital companies), which are more agile.

**Hierarchy:** A lot of companies are still shackled by rigid hierarchical structures that were created for the industrial era, long before digital technology. Digital calls for transforming your structure in line with your strategy. That is, building flexible structures of empowered people always tuned to the changing needs of the market.

**Generality:** In this era of diverse and progressive expectations, a customer product or service plan that is not customizable will rarely work. Each customer must be treated as an individual, and personalization must be intrinsic to your offerings.

**Suppression:** Nothing is a higher barrier to your digital journey than silencing the voice of innovation. Sometimes the best, and the most profitable, ideas come from the most unexpected sources, which would have gone unheard in a climate where innovation was not openly stimulated. A company that does not encourage the dare-to-try spirit does not have a great digital future. I have seen that while professing innovation is common, practicing it, which means embracing its risks and making investments, is not.

## Taking Advantage of the Digital Opportunity

A digital enterprise may either be born digital or be turned digital. Uber, Alibaba, Facebook, Twitter, Grofer, Instacart, Airbnb, and Google are examples of enterprises that were born digital. Interestingly, born-digital companies are some of the fastest growing companies in history, and yet many of them do not own (or stock) the goods or services that they "sell." Such is the power of digital technology. These companies rely on a robust Internet, and a sophisticated supply chain (delivery) system, to reach millions across the globe. They themselves are just extremely thin layers that sit on top of these supply systems. All that they essentially do is *interface* with a vast number of people looking for options at a reasonable price while automating the entire value chain involving supplies, payments, logistics, and service. The value center is clearly shifting from the product to the interface. While this is a compelling business model, digital enterprises that take the *opposite* path have also emerged—they own *all* the layers from R&D to marketing and distribution, thus having greater control and higher profits but also more overheads and challenges in scaling up. Both these types of digital enterprises, however, are examples of companies that were *born* digital. Then there are companies that *turn* digital. The Indian Railways (ticketing system), fast moving consumer goods (FMCG) companies like P&G, e-governments, and banks are among countless examples of institutions that have *turned* digital to embrace the changing times. The questions to ask right now are: were *you* born digital, and if not, have *you* turned digital yet? Do you have a distinct business model to take advantage of the digital opportunity? An enterprise's digital makeover is a continuous journey. Are *you* on that path yet?

The great thing about digital enterprises is that despite the many different models, markets, and ambits, they are all constructed from a similar set of building blocks. These building blocks come together seamlessly in a well-coordinated interplay, creating an inclusive entity that is more than the sum of its parts. A disproportionate focus on technology alone is the commonest reason that many companies fail to reach their potential. It is the seamless integration of technology into a broader ecosystem that is the key to success of a digital enterprise. What are these building blocks, and how do they fit together? To answer this, let us turn to the next chapter.

# CHAPTER 8

# The Making of the Digital Enterprise

There's an American proverb that says, "The only difference between stumbling blocks and stepping stones is the way you use them." It is the same with the building blocks of a digital enterprise. That is, depending on how they are used, the building blocks can be an impediment or an impetus to the evolution and growth of a digital enterprise. Which is why, starting with the same set of building blocks, some enterprises make it big in the digital world, while others struggle. In general, constructing a successful digital enterprise entails harmonious interplay and fine balance among the building blocks depicted in Figure 8.1.

The foundational aspects of culture, innovation, and alignment are embedded *within* the blocks, each of which is pivotal to the construction of the digital enterprise. The higher emphasis on Technology in this chapter is not meant to undermine the importance of other blocks. However, readers who are indifferent to technology may skip the sections on Computing architecture and Software and jump to Next Wave IT without loss of continuity.

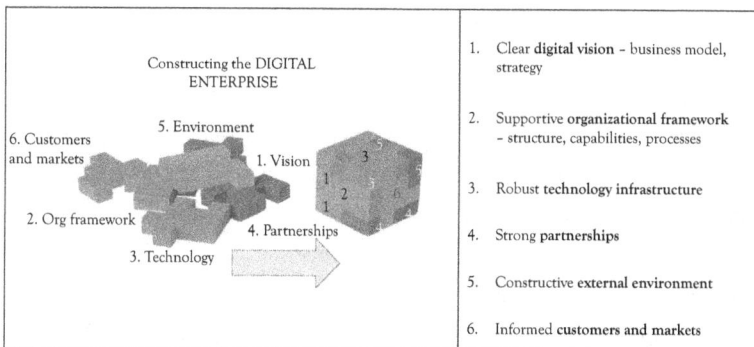

Constructing the DIGITAL ENTERPRISE

6. Customers and markets
5. Environment
1. Vision
2. Org framework
4. Partnerships
3. Technology

1. Clear **digital vision** – business model, strategy

2. Supportive **organizational framework** – structure, capabilities, processes

3. Robust **technology infrastructure**

4. Strong **partnerships**

5. Constructive **external environment**

6. Informed **customers and markets**

*Figure 8.1 Building blocks of a digital enterprise*

## Vision and Strategy

An idea whose time has come is almost always the starting point of a digital enterprise. When the entire organization rallies behind this idea, it forms the vision, or the *seed*, which eventually blossoms into a profitable digital enterprise. Of course, a strong substrate of technology, a supportive structure (capabilities), adaptable processes, and a conducive external environment are critical to transforming the vision into a mature digital enterprise just as soil, climate, photosynthesis, and sunshine are to the metamorphosis of a seed into a fruit-bearing tree.

A seed does not transform into a tree overnight. Similarly, the transformation of a vision into a digital enterprise does not happen instantly. The leadership must ensure that all the nurturing forces are equipped and ready to act upon the idea (vision) in a constructive way.

An *idea* is often born in an isolated setting, perhaps in the shower or on a mountaintop, in the mind of *one* individual. It usually comes as a flash from the blue in a sudden and often jolting way. The *vision*, on the other hand, is created in a collaborative setting to consciously weave an achievable reality around the idea. Thus, when an idea mutates from a solitary spark to a shared inspiration, it becomes a *vision* for the company. It is always a good practice to have a visioning exercise involving as many stakeholders as possible as this creates greater ownership and alignment. If your vision is *seen*, and *believed*, by your entire organization, it has the power to metamorphose your enterprise in an unprecedented way. Think about it—an entire organization of hundreds, or even thousands, of individuals committed to a single belief about making the future happen. Can there be a greater propulsion?

The vision, let's not forget, is the enterprise's image of its *future*. Once you envision a future, you cannot frequently replace it with another image. If the vision of a cement manufacturer is to achieve global dominance by producing high-grade cement that stands out for toughness, this remains its vision even as it goes through changes and upheavals. New technologies may contribute to *realizing* the vision in innovative ways, without *altering* it. However, it is a good practice to reassess your vision as you model yourself into a digital enterprise. But once a vision is decided, all innovation must be directed at its realization, rather than reformulation. Your digital vision, once articulated, must be immune to methods, technologies, and processes adopted to realize it. The vision changes only when the enterprise collectively reimagines its future.

When crafting the digital vision, it is important to keep in mind the end-state of the digital transformation journey. As more advanced technology has become available for bringing ideas to fruition, the timescales for value creation have shortened. For example, with the advent of Hadoop, incorporating Big data into your solution is much faster than earlier. With such accelerators at your disposal, the rubber hits the runway quicker, and this must be reflected in your vision and strategy. Else you risk being outpaced by the market.

When the enterprise embarks upon its digital journey, it must do so with the knowledge that there are frequent and unexpected turns on the path. It is important that these do not diminish the determination or lower the motivation levels. The leaders of the organization must continually reinforce the digital vision and its implications for the company. The value to be gained from the use of digital technologies, and the strategies adopted for engaging with customers and stakeholders, must be clearly seen by *everyone* in the enterprise as necessary conditions for realizing the digital vision.

The *vision* is the organization's image of *who* it intends to become. The *mission* directs the organization to *what* it must do to realize its vision. The *strategies* of all organizational functions stem from this mission, using shared *perspectives*. The strategic goals are commonly derived under Fiscal, Client, External (market), Internal (Process), and Development (Human Capital) perspectives using the *Balanced Score Card*, ensuring that functional strategies complement and reinforce each other.[1]

As is clear from the above, envisioning the future of the digital enterprise is not just about technology. First and foremost, it is about capturing a compelling image of the future in the hearts and minds of the people in the organization.

## Organizational Framework

Your chances of success as a digital enterprise are largely dependent on the people of the organization standing firmly behind the vision and being fully committed to working harmoniously to realize it. The vision, mission, and strategy together ensure that the enterprise is no longer rudderless and is moving forward as a unified force in the desired direction. A good strategy must be able to survive brutal competition, unpredictability, regulatory headwinds, and rising expectations of stakeholders. Therefore, for its accomplishment, the strategy relies on an organizational framework that can adapt to a dynamic external and internal environment.

The organizational framework is the *collective of the structure, capabilities, and processes* designed to execute the company's strategy (Figure 8.2). The organization framework must have the flexibility to adapt to changes in the strategy (say, at the beginning of the business planning cycle), or the business environment itself. Failure to make corresponding changes to the organizational framework with changing strategic focus and market dynamics is a very common, though often intangible, reason for businesses failing to accomplish their stated missions.

The construction of the organizational framework is traditionally done progressively, graduating from one level to the next, focusing simultaneously on the *three* pillars—processes, capabilities, and structure. Table 8.1 provides a high-level view of the properties for each pillar at different levels of maturity. The pillars are interdependent entities and must be taken *together*. That is, a focus on any one of them while ignoring the other two will not lead to targeted results. Each level incorporates the attributes of the preceding one as well. Thus, level 4 processes (metrics-based controls) would include level 2 (repeatability) and level 3 (standardization) processes as well.

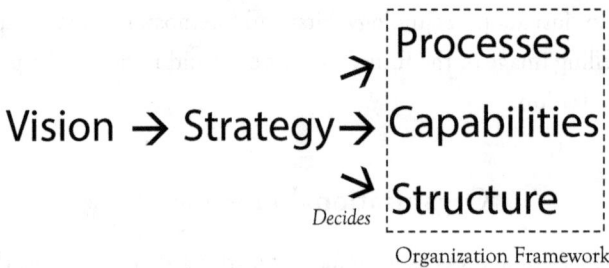

Figure 8.2 Organization framework

*Table 8.1 Organization framework properties*

| Level | Process maturity at | Capabilities focused on | Structure influenced by |
|---|---|---|---|
| 1 | Initial (Mostly situational) | *Individual* competence | *Chain of command* |
| 2 | Repeatable | *Project*/Portfolio expertise | *Team* formation |
| 3 | Standardized | *Functional* excellence | *Functional hierarchy* |
| 4 | Predictable; metrics-based controls | *Customer* (lifecycle) experience | Inverted *pyramid*, voice of customer |
| 5 | Continuously and Measurably Improving | Innovation and differentiation | *Collaboration*, matrix |

Most successful digital enterprises would be in, or targeting to be in, the levels 4 or 5. These are the only levels compatible with the mores of the digital enterprise. Hence any enterprise that is in levels 1 to 3 may find itself struggling to stay afloat in the fast-paced customer-centric world of digital business. The migration through levels is neither quick nor trivial but can be accomplished through consistency of planning and effort to make constructive changes across the three pillars.

Connecting back with our organizational framework, we already made the point above that the target region for successful digital enterprises is in the vicinity of levels 4 and 5. The organizational structure in these levels is influenced by the inverted pyramid and collaboration, respectively. While not going into a detailed treatment of these structures,

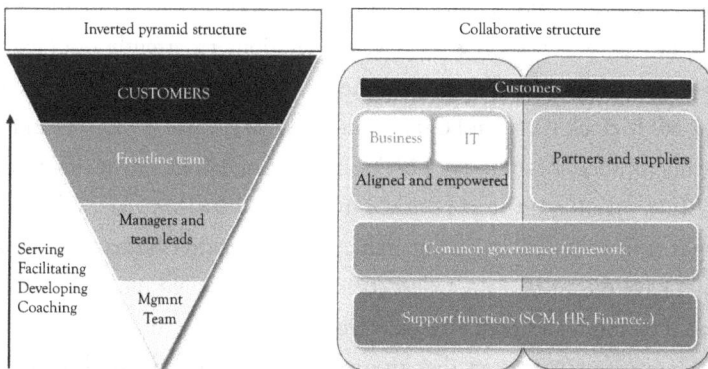

*Figure 8.3 Inverted pyramid and collaborative structure*

a high-level, conceptual view is presented in Figure 8.3 to refresh the reader's understanding.

# Technology

Digital business was ushered by the use of the Internet for connecting enterprises with their customers. Subsequently, the confluence of pervasive connectivity, prolific device ecosystem, data explosion, and Internet Protocol (IP)-centric developments led to innovations like cloud computing, Big data analytics, social media, and enterprise mobility, which form the backbone of a digital business today. At its core, therefore, the digital enterprise represents an unprecedented convergence of business and technology.

### Is Moore's Law Driving Digital Transformation?

For my college project many years ago, I worked on the Intel 8080 microprocessor chip, writing an assembly language program to perform floating-point arithmetic. It was a rather tedious project since assembly language programming entailed writing instructions directly to the microprocessor using hexadecimal nibbles made of 4-bit clumps of 1s and 0s. Nevertheless, it taught me a good deal about the then-emerging field of microprocessors. The 8080 contained about 6,000 transistors woven into a thumbnail-size silicon wafer. Sounded pretty impressive and I recall talking rather animatedly to friends about the marvel that this chip was. Then Moore's law came along, and the 8080 was suddenly left far behind in a fierce race in which successive newer generations recurrently doubled in speed and density of packing, from the 1980s up to the present. Compare the 2 MHz clock speed and 6,000 transistors on the 8080 with the multi-core microprocessors of today with their superfast 4 Giga Hz clock rate and over 1.75 *billion* transistors packed into a thumbnail-size wafer of silicon. To put it in perspective, a comparable growth in other human endeavors would have meant that the tallest structure today would measure halfway up to the moon, and the fastest cars would be nudging the speed of light!

Moore's law predicted that the number of transistors packed into a square inch of an integrated circuit would double every two years—precisely as experience has borne out since the 1980s—resulting in higher computational power from the improved architectures that it enabled. A lot of the advancements in technology that we see around us are a result of Moore's law, including the revolutionary smartphone, which packs more power than a room-sized computer of yore. Indeed, without the strides in IC technology, we would have no foundation to stand on. I foresee that as hardware becomes compacter and faster, it will further drive up *computational power*, or the ability to process complex calculations very quickly. Computational power has been the locomotive of IT in the predigital era. However, could strides in computing power *alone* have led to the evolution of the digital enterprise? Probably not. While IT continues to surge at the same accelerated pace, its drivers have changed. These new drivers, culminating in the evolution of the digital enterprise, define a shift from Moore's law and raw computational power to software, network, and emerging technologies, while hardware still provides the much-needed foundational layer. A digital enterprise must achieve fine-tuning across all these constituents to become and stay successful.

The schematic in Figure 8.4 depicts the major technology drivers of the modern digital enterprise. The architecture itself is supported by a strong *network backbone* to seamlessly interconnect the various modules and components, which are typically *nonlocalized*, and to render mobility and connectivity to the digital enterprise.

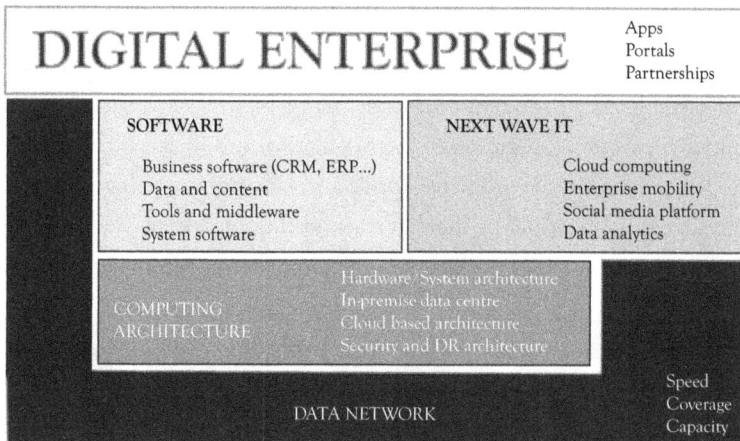

*Figure 8.4 Technology drivers of the digital enterprise*

### Setting the Stage...

Before we proceed further with our discussion on technology, let us revisit a few important points here, which may seem rather obvious but are still worth emphasizing. Incredible as it may seem, issues have snowballed into catastrophes due to such simple matters having been overlooked.

First, having *access* to technology today does not mean *acquiring* (owning or building) the technology. The *proximity* of the hardware components is becoming increasingly less relevant. Hence a digital enterprise may well start life with public cloud infrastructure for all the heavy lifting and publicly available services like Skype or Viber for enhanced communication. Further, the various modules and components of the architecture need not be physically localized. With ubiquitous data connectivity, you can have geographically interspersed components on a single logical plane. This imparts great freedom while designing your architecture. As the enterprise evolves, it will need to reevaluate its stances on data security and privacy and adopt a mix of public and private resources fused seamlessly.

Second, robust *Internet connectivity* lies at the very center of the digital enterprise. Even your most efficient infrastructure is meaningless if your customers, partners, and employees have no access to the Internet. The web is at the very heart of the digital enterprise and permeates all its constituents. Therefore, bridging the digital divide becomes an essential goal of the digital economy, and digital enterprises individually. In countries like India, with a vast population in the rural areas still not having web availability or the means to access it, this presents both an opportunity and a challenge. A modern enterprise may either take the stance that it cannot access this vast chunk of the population and ignore it completely. Or, it can take a more proactive stance and help with ongoing initiatives to bridge the divide and be the first to enter those markets. The following story explains how your outlook can convert a threat into an opportunity.

---

*A reputed shoe manufacturing company in Europe wanted to expand its market to new territories, as it was already well-entrenched in most developed markets. It formed two teams with a mandate to visit an African tribal area and report on the viability of business there. The two teams headed out to this remote region and conducted extensive on-ground research into the potential of the market. On their return to the headquarters, they were both asked to present their findings. The leader of the first team came forward and reported: "There is no market in that area. No one wears shoes." Then the second team was called, and it reported: "There is a huge market in that area. No one wears shoes." Same situation, different perspectives. Who do you think prevailed? These are the kind of situations new enterprises entering uncharted markets frequently come across, and it is their attitude that determines the winners. You may take the back seat and wait for Internet availability or create your own market by ensuring Internet availability.*

### Computing Architecture

The computing architecture is the foundation on which the technology infrastructure of the digital enterprise is built.

A digital business recognizes information, processes, people, and IT systems as entities that participate equally in creating value for the business. The architecture serves as a platform for reliably managing the interplay between the participating entities to assure that all units of the business—while addressing different segments—are delivered the common minimum services to achieve optimum efficiency. A well-designed architecture, like Enterprise Architecture (EA) that we briefly discussed in Chapter 2, also ensures that the enterprise remains agile (responds quickly to change), flexible (can add/modify services on-the-fly), future-ready (caters to evolving trends), and compliant with prevalent standards (interoperable with external systems).

A good starting point for creating the underlying IT architecture for digital business is to establish some non-negotiable ground rules (principles) about the common minimum services that the architecture must offer to all constituents (e.g., business units) of a digital business. Here is a sample list:

- It must be able to *integrate* external devices, programs, components as well as partners and their services through standard application programming interfaces (APIs).

- It should comply with international *standards* of *interoperability* with legacy and future systems.
- The architecture must lend itself to incremental growth strategy, or *scalability*, in line with business growth.
- Users must be able to *access* the business network through maximum possible channels and devices.
- It should expose interfaces that allow *secure* connectivity in compliance with the information privacy norms and policies.
- It should have the capability to acquire and act upon *user-specific data* like location, time of interaction, type of activity, and so on.
- The architecture must allow *interworking* with a variety of data sources and advanced analytic tools for harvesting contextual information from vast repositories.
- It should allow *service creation* and easy *configurability* to support personalization based on user preferences.
- It should enable the adoption of digital best practices and emphasize *customer centricity*.

Standard architecture frameworks like EA and TOGAF specify general rules and guidelines for digital enterprise architecture. They help align IT architecture objectives with business goals for quick and efficient delivery of IT services.

A common understanding and agreement on the fundamental principles governing the architecture is an obvious consequence of Business–IT alignment (BITA). Invest in creating the right computing architecture, as the price of a misstep here could be the derailment of your entire business strategy.

In one of its more common manifestations, the computing architecture for digital enterprises is a synthesis of distinct *modules*, each having a critical role to play in the delivery of digital services. Representative modules constituting the computing architecture are depicted in Figure 8.5, with brief words on the purpose of each module. This composition into independent modules ensures rapid reconfiguration to accommodate new features or services. You do not have to go into the specific design details

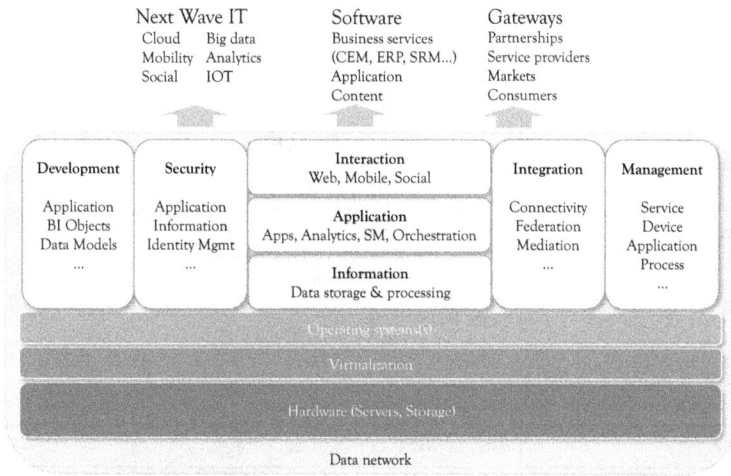

**Figure 8.5  Computing architecture**

of the IT architecture of your enterprise (unless you are an enterprise architect). Most of us only need the big picture.

The architecture must be built for scalability, reliability, and resilience. The business depends on it. It must be ensured that redundancy, disaster recovery, and physical security are adequately factored in its construction. It is also imperative that required skills, tools, and recovery solutions are in place *before* the architecture is rolled out and to certify their currency periodically.

## Software

The term "software" conjures up different images depending on by whom and from where it is viewed. In the view of the microprocessor or Very Large-Scale Integration (VLSI) chip designer, the embedded machine language program using the unique instruction set that controls the behavior of the microprocessor is the software. For a computer programmer, the code written to implement a functionality is software. For most of us who are not computer professionals, the business applications (like CRM or enterprise resource planning (ERP)), productivity tools (like Word or Excel) and the apps downloaded on our devices are software. For some, the controls on the microwave oven are its software! The fact is, everyone is right. Software is a rather generic term today. But that does not

*Table 8.2 Some software categories*

| Software Category | Example |
|---|---|
| Analytics | Cognos, Tableau |
| Antivirus | McAfee, Symantec, Dr Web |
| Architecture | TOGAF, IEEE471, EA (Zachmann) |
| Audio / Music Program | iTunes, WinAmp |
| Configuration | CASE Tools, data modeling |
| Cloud Computing | SaaS, PaaS |
| Data Management | Hadoop |
| Business Intelligence | Data mining, data warehousing, visualization, dashboards |
| Database | Access, MySQL, SQL, Oracle 11g |
| Device Drivers | USB |
| File Transfer | FTP |
| E-mail | Microsoft Outlook, Lotus Notes, Public e-mail (Gmail, Yahoo) |
| Enterprise Services | ERP, CRM, Human Capital Management (HCM) |
| Gaming | Need for Speed, Battlefield4, Modern Combat 5 |
| Information Security | Identity management, authentication, EPS, firewall |
| Internet browser | Google Chrome, Internet Explorer, Mozilla |
| Messaging and Communication | Lync, Skype |
| Mobility | MDM, mobile application (App) development |
| Movie Player | Real Player, VLC, Windows Media Player |
| Navigator | Google Earth, Apple Maps |
| Operating System | Windows XP, MacOS X10, Unix, Linux |
| Photo/Graphic editor | Adobe Photoshop, CorelDRAW |
| Presentation | PowerPoint |
| Programming Language | C++, HTML, Java, Perl, Visual Basic |
| Scripting | VBScript, Jscript, Perl |
| Simulation | Flight simulator, Simcity |
| Spreadsheet | Excel |
| Testing | Test Manager, QA Tools |
| Utility | Data compression, encryption, disk cleanup, backup/restore |
| Web Development | Java Netbeans, HTML editor, Frontpage |
| Word processor | Word |

diminish its power to impact our lives profoundly. In fact, with digital taking over every walk of human life, the share of software in our lives is now bigger than ever before. And increasing.

Software comes in a wide variety of forms—from system software to applications. Anything that is understood by a computer (as an instruction) and can interact with it, and in turn provide users like us a means to exploit its capabilities and perform tasks, is software. Even though both hardware and software are indispensable for a computer system, the current trend is for hardware to become increasingly commoditized while software provides the differentiating functionality. Custom hardware is a fading prospect. An example (from the telecom world) is the trend toward software-defined network elements. Most of the routing function of the Internet is implemented on standard servers (running software) and not specialized routers. The days of dedicated hardware like core switches and routers, base stations, and so on are surely numbered, thanks to leaps in software.

Our search for software products (tools, applications) in our personal and business setting begins with identifying the type and *purpose* of the required software. We then look at the available *options* for that type. Some popular categories of software and a few options against each—chosen for their relevance in the digital context—is presented in Table 8.2. One of the challenges from a software user's perspective is assuring that the software product and version is the most up-to-date. Obsolescence can hurt your business. You can either buy software outright or, as is more prevalent in the digital world, *license* its use for a specified period. The latter option assures that you stay current with version upgrades. However, strict compliance with licensing terms is essential, as even inadvertent breach of intellectual property rights could have disastrous legal consequences.

One of the most critical tasks that an enterprise would undertake in its maturation is defining and implementing its software landscape. This is a function of the present state of IT systems and processes in your company, the future direction of the company, investment capacity, and market dynamics, among others. It is not a task that can be done and dusted away in a single effort. The software landscape includes changes, new implementations, upgrades, consolidations, and reassessments that go on throughout the lifespan of the enterprise. Deep commitment and involvement of all stakeholders, with IT steering the enterprise around bottlenecks and inefficiencies, is a must at every stage.

The software landscape designers must work on at least five different layers, depicted in Figure 8.6. Each layer calls for a different set of competencies and focus. The layers must be designed such that they fit together

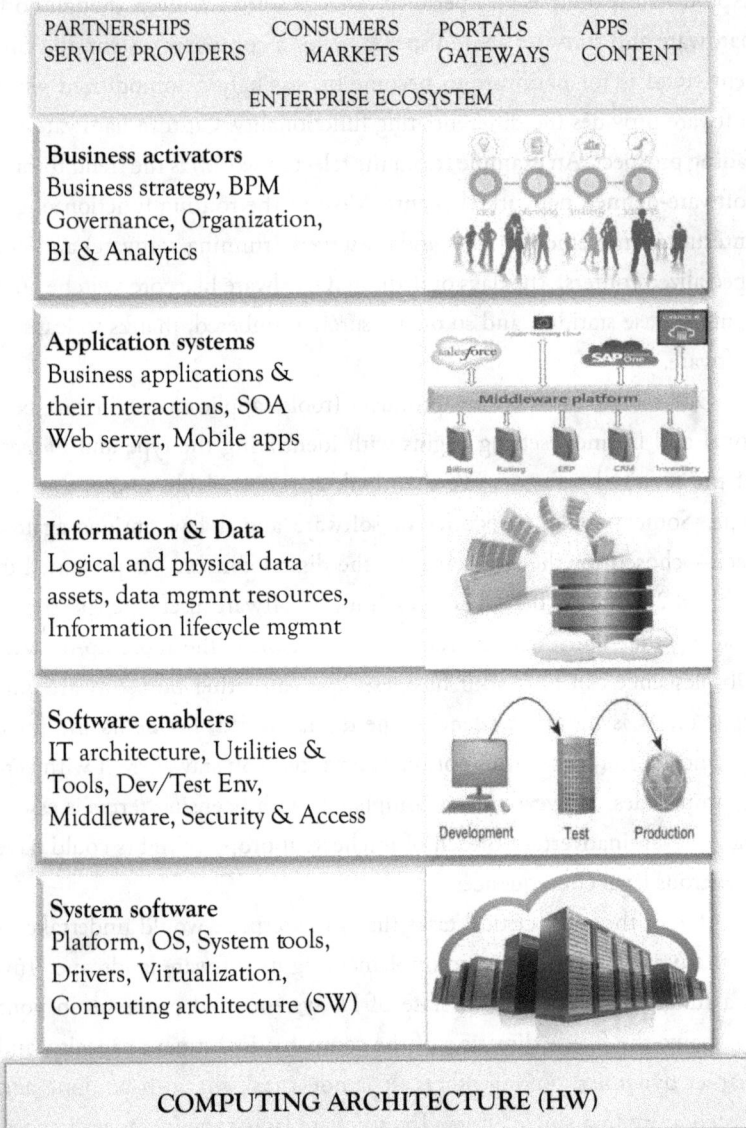

| PARTNERSHIPS | CONSUMERS | PORTALS | APPS |
| SERVICE PROVIDERS | MARKETS | GATEWAYS | CONTENT |

ENTERPRISE ECOSYSTEM

**Business activators**
Business strategy, BPM
Governance, Organization,
BI & Analytics

**Application systems**
Business applications &
their Interactions, SOA
Web server, Mobile apps

**Information & Data**
Logical and physical data
assets, data mgmnt resources,
Information lifecycle mgmnt

**Software enablers**
IT architecture, Utilities &
Tools, Dev/Test Env,
Middleware, Security & Access

Development     Test     Production

**System software**
Platform, OS, System tools,
Drivers, Virtualization,
Computing architecture (SW)

**COMPUTING ARCHITECTURE (HW)**

*Figure 8.6 Enterprise software building blocks*

seamlessly and smoothly and are also able to interact easily with the surrounding environment consisting of the network, computing architecture including the hardware platform, and the emerging technology ecosystem consisting of cloud, social, mobile, Big data, and perhaps Internet of Things (IoT), Web 2.0, Artificial Intelligence (AI), and others down the road. Software is nothing if not scalable and adaptable.

A technical discussion covering all the myriad aspects of software engineering involved in constructing the enterprise landscape would be neither possible nor justified here.

Many of the new software applications in use today are mobile apps, that is, software for which the client runs on mobile devices. The front-end mobile apps work on the user device while at the backend they run on enterprise systems, some of which may be legacy. Building your software landscape for the future may not require sun-setting all your legacy systems. It is an incremental or phased, approach wherein elements are retired and refreshed in layers. Invest time in planning this well, and you will discover that it is entirely possible to coincide your new acquisitions of software and hardware with the end-of-life timeline of your legacy systems (which would anyway have necessitated an upgrade or a refresh). That way, you spread your costs over a length of time and avoid a deep dent in your budget.

A common question companies ask themselves is whether to buy the software off the shelf or to build it as per the internal requirements of the company. Most commercially available software is customizable to individual requirements, and I strongly advocate going for commercial off-the-shelf (COTS) software by default. The interface challenges (e.g., keeping up with future requirements) entailed in *bespoke* software outweigh the comfort of tailored development in most cases. The following example will explain my reasons for this proclivity.

---

**Example 8.1**

*A few years ago, I was part of a working group to assess the reasons behind a group company's repeated slippages of time-to-market commitments for new launches, and failure to bring products that could sharpen its competitive edge. The company was falling behind in its ability to fulfill customer orders, deliver committed levels of service, and bill customers for services. After a lot of internal deliberation, it was concluded that the root cause was the company's IT systems. An independent assessment was called for, and this working group was created with a mandate to diagnose the specific causes.*

*The company's IT systems were implemented about eight years ago. Barring some user applications like office productivity tools, e-mail, and so on, its entire software architecture was made up of bespoke (custom-made) systems that were uniquely adapted to the company's business environment of eight years ago. What was not entirely homegrown was so heavily customized that it was difficult to distinguish it from homegrown development. All too often, business requirements would either change or give way to entirely new ones. In such events, Business would approach the IT team with change requests (CRs) mostly capturing at a high-level what business had in mind. Based on these CRs, the IT team would either develop or (rarely) buy new software and customize it to fit in the environment. This system had been perfected to an art form in the company. As many as 100 CRs were being implemented each month!*

*What we, the working group, discovered was that eight years later, the system was crumbling under the weight of these CRs. The overall performance had become sluggish, and for the last two years, the system was on the brink of collapse. There were many islands of CRs working outside the main architecture. There was also no standard integration across the incrementally (CR by CR) built modules. Version mismatches abounded, which inhibited interactions. Elements were somehow glued together to interwork, even when they were noncompatible. In many cases, Original Equipment Manufacturer (OEM) support was not available due to heavy customization. Documentation for the countless CRs was inadequate. There was heavy dependence on the original coder, who was always elusive. Bug fixes and patches overlaid the code almost entirely. These problems had reduced the software architecture to a parody of its original avatar to the extent that it was no longer able to cater to routine business expectations of performance and functionality. When we presented the detailed findings to the management, there was pin-drop silence in the room for about 30 seconds. Then the CFO spoke up, "Can we do anything now or we have to close shop?"*

*Well, we did have our recommendation on redesigning the IT landscape and bringing in a better, more modular structure to the IT systems, but the dominant lesson for everyone was that overdependence on bespoke software, in the long run, was disastrous. Unlike COTS, homegrown software does not lend itself to automatic upgrades and migrations to keep it current, nor does it offer the level of standardization that is required to interface with the external world. If you are a closed system unto yourself, like a NASA rocket mission to Saturn, you can go the bespoke way. But for a business enterprise in a dynamic environment and catering to a plethora of external agencies, I always recommend the COTS route with carefully planned and minimal changes to the original code. Changes that can be accomplished by adjusting the configurable parameters in the software are fine. But those that require changes to its code are an invitation to disaster in the long run.*

Transforming your software and systems to meet the evolving requirements of the digital enterprise is a carefully planned and monitored process. Applications and software need to be transformed in accordance with the business landscape. The term "digital transformation" is commonly used to describe the enterprise's journey from the traditional to the digital. It is a nontrivial exercise involving the conversion of software architecture from the patchy and nonstandard specimen like the one described in the previous example, to a more decentralized and modular one in which the various modules are independent and interactive, like service-oriented architecture (SOA). To conform to the changed architecture, and to bring flexibility and agility, your old, or legacy, *applications* also need to be modernized. This could require a revamping of the source code to modern platforms such as C# and .NET. Some applications may need to be reengineered for new functionalities, and new and friendlier user interfaces may have to be built that are supported across different platforms and devices. If you have a sizeable IT infrastructure, it is best to engage a digital transformation consultant to advise you on the quickest path, which may entail not just modernization of your applications and architecture but also seamless interworking with newer age IT solutions that are defining the digital landscape in the modern business world.

### Next-Wave IT

I thought long and hard for a term to use for all the new technological advancements that are becoming a part of our lives and yet cannot be uniquely classified under the existing building blocks of technology like software, network, or computing architecture. We are familiar with social, mobile, analytics, and cloud, collectively known by their acronym SMAC, and I toyed with this. But the field is emerging so fast that soon we may have other, more powerful technologies becoming dominant to which the term SMAC will not do justice. Take IoT, for example, or 3D printing. Or for that matter, smart-everything (smart devices, homes, cities, planet), AI, and robotics. I am very sure that these—and their intersections—will become as much a part of the digital ecosystem as SMAC over time. I finally settled on the term Next-Wave IT to describe all such new advances in technology, built from familiar blocks but profound and pervasive in their impact. Much of our current discussion on digital enterprises may still focus on SMAC, but it is important to be mindful that the digital ecosystem is an expanding one.

A question very often asked in the context of emerging technologies is about the specific role of these technologies in the construction and running of the digital enterprise. It is impossible to answer this question comprehensively. Every digital enterprise envisages a new way of leveraging these technologies to suit its business model.

A few years ago, I set up an application to host my catalog of books on the cloud. I invited some friends, book lovers all, to add their collection of books too, and soon we had a sizeable cloud-based library. The application, which could be run from a smartphone, allowed us to select and "reserve" books, which we exchanged with each other during weekly get-togethers over beer or coffee. It was a very simple application but served our purpose well.

In the above simple example, we have several elements of SMAC at play. There is a cloud storage where all the catalogs were published by individual members, there is a social interaction between the members using a messaging platform (a popular social app), and there is mobility that enables access to information from everywhere, using a mobile app run on smartphones.

This is a very elementary case, but it shows  how social media, mobility, and Cloud can come together to ignite the enterprise spirit and boost collaboration. The only private ingredient required above is a Java program to implement a basic mobile application hosted on a home computer connected to the Internet, which doubles up as a web server. The obvious question here is then the following: If all it takes to create and run a digital enterprise is Next-Wave IT or SMAC, then why invest in complex IT systems? Unfortunately, life is not as simple as my book club. A typical enterprise of even medium size would need systems to manage its internal workflows (like enterprise resource planning (ERP)), run customer service operations (using CRM and other IT tools), manage its order processing, payments/collections and fulfillment streams, run marketing campaigns, and manage its internal operations involving people (HR), supply chain (SCM), financial planning, and such. There are, of course, myriad other considerations ranging from productivity tools to data warehouses, foundational computing power, security, disaster recovery, and so on, which involve IT systems. In larger enterprises, the IT substrate penetrates even deeper. For a thriving digital ecosystem, the computing architecture and the software must integrate and *interwork* with Next-Wave IT and together create enhanced value for the business.

A lot of us think of digital enterprises as ones that interact with their customers only through an app or portal, while its people remain faceless and anonymous. Indeed, we mentioned one of the characteristics of digital enterprises as "Use of digital channels (web, mobile, social) for engagement with customer thru lifecycle." However, it is important to emphasize that Next-Wave IT is not a substitute for the human touch. It just opens more avenues and touchpoints to connect. Some enterprises in fact, use Next-Wave IT very effectively to expand their business while strengthening their people-to-people relationships at the same time.

**Example 8.2**

*A few months ago, I interviewed a business manager of a multi-billion-dollar software services company on the adoption of Next-Wave IT for selling and delivering services to a global client base in a high-tech high-touch scenario. Following is the gist of what he passionately shared with me.*

*As the first step, his company established innovation centers for incubating digital technology solutions collaboratively with customers. The innovation center focuses on bringing the benefits of technologies like mobility, Cloud computing, and Big data to enterprise customers across industry segments.*

*Next, this company has built unique capabilities in digital transformation based on its extensive experiences globally, spawning a distinct consulting practice to help customers with their digital and social media strategy, marketing analytics, and experience management.*

*As a global player, it has also fostered local and global alliances with technology partners to enrich its offerings and enhance its capability to offer end-to-end digital solutions.*

*Apart from cultivating skills and partnerships in the Next-Wave IT technologies, it has built its own Cloud-based offerings, which provide customers quick and cost-effective solutions in a multitenancy mode.*

*All through these initiatives, the overarching aim is to enable customers to reimagine their businesses and help them seamlessly transform to digital.*

*Over the last two years, they have emerged among the most trusted technology partners globally for enterprises going digital.*

*Sounds like a sales pitch, doesn't it? Well, it probably isn't, going by the track record and customer references. Anyhow, the point is that this is a large company that is enabling digital transformation by itself practicing what it advocates and implements for its customers.*

*The internal environment here buzzes with high-tech. BYOD is strongly encouraged, and most of its intranet is accessible over employees' mobile phones. Its employees routinely log in to their work or leisure activities in the company-run Wi-Fi enabled buses on their way to/from work.*

*Most of the company's data and programs—like its ERP, financial systems, human capital management (HCM), and so on.—are hosted on a hybrid cloud, which incorporates solutions from its technology partners. It leverages Big data and analytics to provide real-time information to employees and stakeholders on a range of issues in an incredibly intuitive fashion. There is a thriving social network of its own, which is at the fingertips of each one of its over a hundred thousand employees across the globe. It helps employees connect on issues ranging from sharing of accommodation to help on customer problems through focus groups. Even the process of account management is digitized with online information on customers' entire portfolio, people, and projects. They are also building an Artificial Intelligence layer to supplement some of their backend shared services. When a prospective client scouting for a digital transformation partner visits their facility, the deal is half done while just walking through the aisles.*

There are four primary reasons behind enterprises embracing SMAC for business. The first is *connectivity,* or the ease of networking among ecosystem participants. The second is *collaboration,* or the ability to come to a common platform for transacting business and sharing experiences. The third is *freedom,* that is, not being dependent on a specific device, platform, network, or location for engaging in a business activity. And the fourth is *empowerment,* or ready and direct access to relevant information by those who need it, when they need it. Underlying these advantages is the enormous *convenience* that SMAC offers to the participants of the enterprise ecosystem through simple, new, and exciting ways of doing business.

In Chapter 3, we explored SMAC as a central fixture in the new IT landscape. Let us quickly reassess the pivotal part played by SMAC in the operation of a digital business.

**Social:** Be it socializing or social networking, social is in the human DNA. At no point in history have social traits shown a declining trend, and this is not likely in the future as well, with technology making things more expedient than ever. Social is about engaging people in something they care about, and digital businesses have leveraged this human trait brilliantly to expand their reach. Businesses are now using social as an indispensable source of insightful data on customer behavior and sentiment for their marketing and design purposes.

**Mobile:** We are a people on the go. With the proliferation of mobile devices and ubiquity of wireless networks, we are no longer subject to the restrictions of time and place to conduct our business. As we said, mobility is not just about movement. It is about *freedom*. With more mobile devices than people in the world and with over three out of every five of those devices having "smart" capabilities, businesses must necessarily transform themselves to enable their consumers to cash in on this freedom. Or perish.

**Analytics:** We talked about the data revolution earlier. There are startling statistics on the speed, size, and types of data that we as a populace are generating and consuming each day on social and mobile platforms. This data is now recognized as an indisputable *business asset*. Our ability to analyze this Big data—irrespective of its volume, velocity, and variety—and garner deep insights into preferences, behaviors, and sentiment will decide, in ever increasing ways, our survival chances in the digital economy.

**Cloud:** For the consumers, cloud implies that all the heavy lifting—running complex programs, storing huge volumes of data—is no longer the burden of their device. A $100 smartphone can "run" almost any program and access unlimited content. And you can switch to any other device at any time and still get the same experience with no loss of processing-power or content. For the enterprise, cloud means avoidance of substantial investments in premise-based equipment and technology, freedom from maintenance, and the ability to offer quick setup times (reduced time-to-market) to the business.

As we have seen above and before, each element of SMAC has compelling advantages for business. However, the real breakthrough happens from their coming *together* as *intersecting elements*. Enterprises can maximize their impact through the innovative use of these intersections. For example, using *Big data analytics* to gauge customer sentiments expressed about the company's products over *social media*; using *Cloud-based* content to enable seamless experience for *mobile* users when they are in another city, country, or continent; accessing *Cloud-based* data to get information on a mobile (on-the-go) user and combine the preferences derived through *Big data analytics* with *location* information to recommend places of interest in the vicinity, like book stores, restaurants, and so on.

Look at a digital enterprise as a symphony where the individual SMAC elements are the musical instruments, each of which can produce a beautiful rendition of its own, but when they come *together* as an ensemble, magic happens. It is up to you, the conductor of the symphony, to orchestrate the digital concert and set the right rhythm and tempo, which will keep your audiences enthralled.

There are innumerable ways in which Next-Wave IT, including SMAC, can be an asset for your business. We may not be able to enumerate every possible benefit to every business here. It would be best to do this in your own environment as a brainstorming exercise. To set the tempo, here are five pointers that may apply to your business:

- SMAC offers global reach—Companies that adopt SMAC can tap into new markets more easily.
- SMAC promotes collaboration—It provides limitless opportunities for enterprises to engage with customers, understand their preferences, and offer custom solutions.

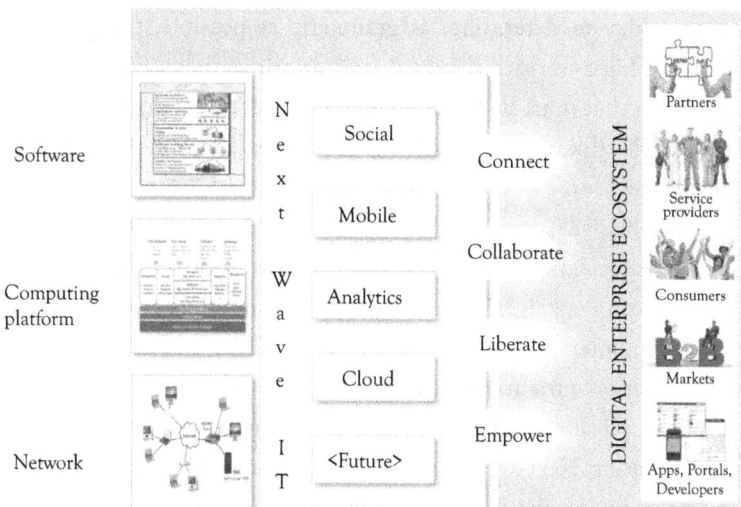

*Figure 8.7 Next-wave IT*

- SMAC enhances the customer experience—By analyzing behaviors and trends, SMAC makes it possible to personalize offerings and preempt problems, thus promoting customer loyalty.
- SMAC is a great leveler—SMAC levels the playing field for enterprises and customers alike. Every business has access to all customers, and vice versa.
- SMAC boosts productivity—With the level of empowerment, freedom, and access to information enabled by SMAC, enterprises that adopt SMAC achieve far higher workforce productivity.

Next-Wave IT can be built incrementally, that is, investment of time and money in building the Next-Wave IT infrastructure can be aligned closely to the business growth, and thus there is minimal risk of going over-the-line with your costs.

Like all enterprise initiatives, Next-Wave IT must have a clearly stated goal for its implementation. For example, the goal could be *to improve upsell revenues through contextual and instantaneous connect with customers* (here, *contextual* would require Big data analytics to garner preferences, and *instantaneous* would require social media access, unrestricted by time and place). Once your goal is defined, study where you are today to determine, as granularly as possible, the gaps that need to be filled to reach this goal, and prioritize these. Each gap is an action item that must be tracked and completed. There may be certain dependencies (like cost and skills) in closing specific actions, that need to be planned for.

Companies that can best leverage SMAC are able to manage their customer information, interfaces, and experiences in the most optimal way. They can congregate customer data from multiple channels (social media [SM], interactive voice response [IVR], CRM, and so on) and keep the information current and relevant. They set up systems and processes to avoid  duplication and deficiency of information.

In adopting Next-Wave IT for your company, a *dedicated* team to assess its potential, and focus on maximizing its use in your environment would be a better idea than spreading the responsibility too widely. It is also recommended to keep scouting for best practices of other successful organizations and plan to blend these into your environment. There is still evolution happening in this field, and hence, there is an excellent scope for learning from peers.

When we started out on our segment on Next-Wave IT, we mentioned that it is built of SMAC and *other* disruptive technologies that have great potential that we are only beginning to tap. These are the technologies that are waiting to take hold of the Future box in Figure 8.7. Let us consider one such in a short example and reflect on the consequences on business when this intersects with some existing technologies.

*We are familiar with the digitization of information in today's world, which essentially means reducing text, images, sound, and video into a string of binary digits that can be stored, processed, analyzed, transmitted, and manipulated. Look at the revolution this has brought. Now think of digitization not just of information, but of matter itself! That is, the possibility that you can store, process, analyze, transmit, and regenerate physical objects using the same software principles that were applied to information! 3D Printing, as the digitization of matter is referred to, is poised for a tremendous impact on the future of business and society. It is no longer about simple toys and tools. It is expected that the first 3D-printed car will be on the road by 2023. Even more astonishingly, the first transplant of the 3D-printed liver may happen as early as 2025! With 3D printing, you can do your personalized object design and production, thus closing the gap between product creator and user. Instead of waiting for an ordered item to be delivered to you, just press Ctrl-P and presto, it is there—made for you! There are, of course, some sinister and worrisome implications of 3D printing as well—some may use this to mass produce weapons and counterfeits, even spurious human organs. New forms of security, control mechanisms, and ethical protocols will no doubt evolve to counter this threat. There are many profound questions that mainstreaming of 3D printing raises. However, as a technological breakthrough, it is indeed a giant step. And it is only one among several contenders (think IoT, smart planet, and so on) for the Future box in our Next-Wave IT depiction. Exciting times ahead.*

It is very common for people to ask at this stage if technology will replace humans as the world becomes increasingly digital. In my view, the answer is no. Technology, in fact, has recently *created* more jobs than any other discipline and it will continue to do so. The amount of displacement—or the difference between repetitive roles *eliminated* and new ones *created*—will always be in favor of humans. However, I will say this: While technology will not replace people, *it is certain that people who understand and can use technology will replace those who cannot.*

## Partnerships

In my several years of working with digital enterprises at various stages of evolution, I have not come across even one example of a digital enterprise that did not rely on partnerships to conduct its business. A digital enterprise is not a company but an ecosystem. It rests on the premise that one company is not the undisputed champion in every area of its business operation and therefore to leverage the expertise of other companies—even those that you may be competing with—in their specific domains makes sound business sense. In fact, we have many examples of companies having no core competence in the area that they dominate their markets in, but their ability to manage networks of partners and weave them into their business model has spelled their success. They are called aggregators.

Aggregation is not the only form of partnership known to digital enterprises. Depending on the size and nature of the enterprise, the partnerships may differ. Almost every element of the digital enterprise is amenable to partnerships. A digital enterprise stems from an idea or vision, and that is all that is truly integral to the enterprise. With value chains becoming more complex as customers expect complete solutions from one source, the extent and role of partnering are becoming an increasingly core aspect of strategic planning in digital enterprises. In other words, partnerships are a matter of corporate strategy and cannot surface (or submerge) randomly.

Partnerships require nurturing and management. Your business depends on it. It is not just a matter of placing controls and management dashboards. There is also *trust* to be invested from both sides. The whole

**Figure 8.8  The extended digital enterprise**

process of partner management is usually quite complex though many companies believe it to be trivial. It is *never* safe to assume that one can "partner and forget." A partnership is an extension of your enterprise, which rids you of certain routine overheads but also brings in responsibilities and risks that need to be managed carefully. It is very important to remember that *your partner is invisible to the external world.* You must own the consequences of any deficiencies in service, legal infringements, and so on and their impact on your hard-built reputation. No customer (or court) will accept the plea that it was your partner's fault. Therefore, in managing your partnerships, avoid suspicion but never drop caution.

Figure 8.8 illustrates the most common kinds of partnerships constituting the *extended* digital enterprise. Managing these partnerships is the lifeline of the digital enterprise. Generally, each partnership comes with its own contractual frameworks, key result areas (KRAs), and service level agreements (SLAs), which need to be closely monitored.

---

**Example 8.3**

*Typically, mobile companies are not at their best when it comes to stocking and dispensing music to suit the individual tastes of their millions of users. On the other hand, users today are no longer content with the canned set of ringtone options that come with their device. Whom do people turn to for fulfilling these wants? Yes, the mobile service operator. Though this is a seemingly trivial requirement, it is not within the core competence of most operators. So, operators turn to partners for rendering this service. These partners build the required logic for delivering the selected music to the individual user, host the service on behalf of the operator, and provide necessary integrations to enable provisioning, de-provisioning, charging, and so on. Further, these service partners rely on a different entity called the content partner for providing a continuously updated supply of music choices to the user. This is a familiar instance of a seamless, invisible chain of partnerships enhancing the delivery capability of a larger, more visible, customer-facing enterprise (the mobile operator). The customer-facing enterprise must take ownership of the quality and conduct of the invisible partners and face the music of a different genre when things don't work for customers!*

Strong partnerships are the invisible driving force behind the digital enterprise. They make the enterprise more wholesome and attractive. A digital enterprise is essentially a *network* of blended companies, presenting a single window to the world.

## Influencers

We live in a regulated environment. Almost every industry—telecom, retail, insurance, banking, health care—is governed by a set of regulations that it must comply with. The regulator can—and often does—demand regular as well as exceptional reports on a range of parameters relating to the company's operation and its compliance to the commitments and rules based on which it sold goods and services to its clients. The digital enterprise is not excepted from regulation. It must, therefore, conduct a detailed assessment of the regulation and the steps required to comply with those regulations in a demonstrable way. Unlike with partners, most enterprises have an arms-length relationship with regulators. Here the determinant of success is not collaboration but compliance.

Almost every enterprise must interwork with its peer companies in the industry. For example, banks work with other banks for interbank transactions, and telecom companies have interconnect settlements with other telecom companies for roaming and call completion. Peer companies must connect to a universal *gateway* through which the intercompany transactions are routed. A digital enterprise must expose standard interfaces to the requisite gateways to assure its subscription to the industry network, and thus avoid isolation.

It is usual for industries to have associations consisting of individual companies as members. These associations are powerful bodies that formulate the rules of engagement and are a guard against unfair practices by one of its members or outside forces. They play an indispensable role in guiding and influencing government policies for the industry. As digital enterprises are at an emerging stage, some of these practices are in a relatively fluid state at present. There are few, if any, active countrywide associations of digital enterprises belonging to an industry. However, over time, there will be greater regulation, government involvement, and public participation, which would necessitate strong industrywide associations of digital enterprises as well.

With the advent of social media, customers have a new way of expressing their opinion about any aspect of an enterprise. It is easier for negative sentiment, or bias against one company, to transcend the one-on-one communication between the company and the customer and reach thousands of other customers. These customers may, in turn, come together against the enterprise and collectively escalate the matter, resulting in avoidable negative publicity. In order to protect their interests, digital enterprises must have access to impartial nodal agencies to look after their interest, singly and jointly.

There are many such instances that mandate a seamless merger of the digital enterprise with its external environment. The enterprise must align with its competitors, customer forums, government bodies, and other influencers to reach consensus on pricing, quality, and service levels and therefore it is essential that it stays "plugged-in."

Lastly, an enterprise, digital or not, is part of the broader community to which it owes its existence. This broader community is the canvas of educational institutions, hospitals, utility services, nonprofit organizations, environmental lobbies, and society in general from which the enterprise has benefitted and to which it must give back. This may be in the form of various contributions including monetary donations, participation in development work, espousing a charitable cause, or extending aid. A digital enterprise must recognize that as much as it exists to generate business and profits, it has a responsibility toward the society of which it is a part.

## Markets and Consumers

Some things do not change even with major economic, technological, and social upheavals. To exist, businesses, including digital ones, need customers. Managing the experiences of customers, who are *people*, is on the critical path for digital enterprises as well.

A customer is someone who has the financial power to *demand* what the company is offering, and the *set of all customers with a similar demand and all sellers who can fulfill that demand constitutes a market.*

Many of the essential tenets of marketing are unaltered by digital technology. The advent of digital technology has spawned the field of *digital marketing*, or the innovative use of technology to understand and influence consumer buying behavior. I find it quite amusing that digital marketing is itself being marketed as a discipline to be taught in classrooms! The company's marketing and technology teams putting their heads together to find creative solutions is the surest way to influence customers. In other words, *a strong BITA equals a sound digital marketing strategy.* The digital marketing strategy is unique to an enterprise and is a function of its technological prowess and vision of the future (Figure 8.9).

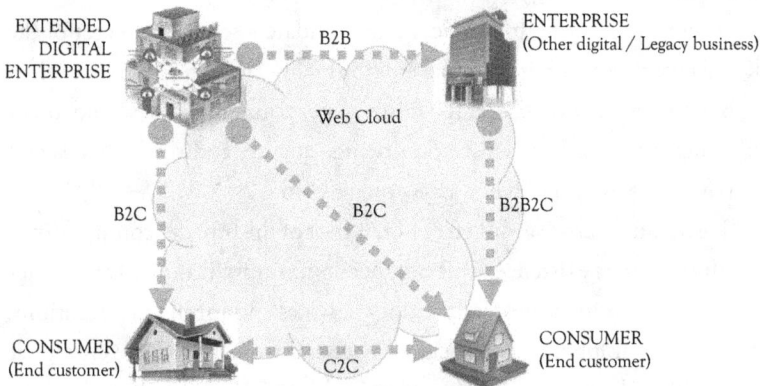

*Figure 8.9 Markets and consumers*

A digital marketing strategy is focused on generating maximum engagement with customers, often using high-quality interactive content accessed through various social media platforms like Facebook, LinkedIn, Twitter, Instagram, Snapchat, and others. The two-way channel allows instant feedback on the perception of the brand among the targeted user base. For example, a leading life insurance company in India launched a creative campaign on Facebook and Twitter to relate real-life stories on how most accidents are not the victims' fault, instantly touching an emotional chord among its audience, and generating awareness of how an insurance policy could benefit everyone. The company provided a simple social media link through which its audience could instantly connect with the company. There was an immediate and measurable upsurge in conversions. In another creative example of digital marketing, a leading hotel at a beach resort in India launched a campaign to promote features that made the hotel appealing to *kids*. The hotel got some social media influencers to experience the hotel and share their experiences over Twitter and Instagram, thus creating awareness of the offerings and attraction among families. The hotel also ran contests on Facebook to boost engagement and drive up bookings. It worked, and the hotel had a 100 percent booking during the entire holiday season!

The future clearly belongs to those who can use the power of digital technology to reach their markets and customers faster. Sounds the obvious thing to do? Well, it is not that obvious to some, as the following example brings out.

---

**Example 8.4**

*This case refers to a sizeable financial services company, a clear leader in its market segment. At the outset of a meeting with the IT leadership team and some external consultants at their posh headquarters, the COO made it clear that the company had failed to capitalize on technology for promoting the business, while their competition had been successful. This shook the audience a bit, as the company was a market leader that one associated with sophistication and expert use of technology. The COO asked the IT team and the external consultants to work together in salvaging the situation and helping them get the business back on track.*

*Two weeks later, the group came up with its assessment. Over the years this company had been gathering data from its customers through transaction records, and customer relationship management (CRM) interactions, and had various IT systems in place to capture and store this information. The problem was that the story ended here. This data had never been accessed, save for some mandated deep diving into a customer's history in cases of legal dispute, and no one quite knew what to do with it. Meanwhile, smaller companies in competition with this company recognized the asset value of the data they generated and used it for more personalized service to customers. What was even more frustrating was that two years ago, there had been a request for investing in advanced analytic systems, which had been turned down as an "extravagant" measure and the funds were used to install a telepresence system! Had this company recognized the power of Big data and advanced analytics at the right time, they would have been in an entirely different league today, certainly not struggling to stay ahead of competitors once considered inconsequential. They accepted the findings and resolved to change course. There is an earnest effort underway to deploy the right technology tools to exploit the power of Big data, training has been imparted to both Business and IT folks on the use of analytics, and the reach of data gathering has been extended to social media. Still, they may never fully reclaim the territory lost due to their failure to recognize the power of digital technology in time.*

The nature of a digital enterprise lends itself to several marketing modes. A digital enterprise may conduct business with another *enterprise* (digital or other), as in the case of a technology company like Microsoft licensing its software products to a bank, law firm, or hospital. This mode is the Business to Business, or B2B in short. What we as individuals most commonly come across is the Business-to-Consumer, or B2C mode, where the digital enterprise conducts business directly with the end customer. Examples, of course, include you and me ordering the latest paperback from Amazon, or booking a cab through Uber. We also have a mode where the digital enterprise sells to another digital enterprise, which, in turn, conducts business with the end-customer or consumer. This mode, referred to as Business-to-Business-to-Consumer, or B2B2C, is an e-commerce model for reaching new markets and customers. Companies selling white-labeled products to other companies that bundle them with their own (e.g., MVNOs), are also an example of B2B2C. Lastly, there is the C2C mode, where one consumer sells to another consumer using digital channels. In most cases, C2C transactions are facilitated by an unseen empowering enterprise. A typical example would be selling pre-used items through an *agent* like OLX or renting out your apartment through CommonFloors.

## In Conclusion...

A digital enterprise is not a massive powerhouse of complex systems and equipment controlled by experts with pointed ears whom the organization must depend on for delivering some esoteric, magical outcomes. At its heart are regular people who dared to try, and never stopped believing that they could accomplish great things. It is made up of uncomplicated building blocks that fit together seamlessly. Standing on a bedrock of strong BITA, each block adds unique strength to the digital edifice. A successful digital enterprise recognizes that *each* building block is crucial to its growth and survival, and never loses sight of one for another. This simple, yet powerful, lesson has been at the root of many a digital success story.

In studying each block of the digital enterprise, you would not have failed to appreciate the growing role of BITA in ensuring enterprise success. Be it strategy, organization, processes, technology, partnerships, or markets, it is no longer Business OR Technology but very strongly Business AND Technology that is going to make it happen for you. Business cannot go it alone in this environment, and nor can Technology. In successful digital organizations, business and technology are fully synchronized or integrated. They are, in fact, indistinguishable. The cultivation of a strong BITA must be among the organization's foremost strategic and operational priorities. It is not only about gaining a competitive edge in the future. It is about surviving long enough to witness the future.

# Acronyms

| | |
|---|---|
| 3-D | Three-Dimensional |
| AI | Artificial Intelligence |
| APAC | Asia Pacific |
| API | Application Programming Interface |
| App | Application |
| AR | Augmented Reality |
| ARPA | Advanced Research Projects Agency |
| ARPU | Average Revenue Per User |
| ATM | Automatic Teller Machine |
| B2B | Business-to-Business |
| B2C | Business-to-Consumer |
| BA | Business Analyst |
| BCI | Brain–Computer Interface |
| BFSI | Banking, Financial Services, and Insurance |
| BI | Business Intelligence |
| BITA | Business–IT Alignment, or Business–Technology Alignment |
| BPM | Business Process Management |
| BTS | Base Transceiver Station |
| BVIT | Business Value of IT |
| BYOD | Bring Your Own Device |
| CAF | Customer Acquisition Form |
| CDO | Chief Digital Officer |
| CDR | Call Data Record |
| CEM | Customer Experience Management |
| CEO | Chief Executive Officer |
| CIO | Chief Information Officer |
| CLC | Customer Lifecycle |
| CLM | Customer Lifecycle Management |
| CM | Configuration Manager |

| | |
|---|---|
| CMM | Capability Maturity Model |
| CMO | Chief Marketing Officer |
| COO | Chief Operating Officer |
| COTS | Commercial Off-the-Shelf |
| CPE | Customer Premise Equipment |
| CPU | Central Processing Unit |
| CR | Change Request |
| CRBT | Caller Ring Back Tone |
| CRM | Customer Relationship Management |
| C-SAT | Customer Satisfaction |
| CSP | Cloud Service Provider |
| CTO | Chief Technology Officer |
| DBA | Database Administrator |
| DR | Disaster Recovery |
| e2e | End-to-end |
| EA | Enterprise Architecture |
| EB | Exa Bytes |
| EDP | Electronic Data Processing |
| ENIAC | Electronic Numerical Integrator and Computer |
| EOY | End of Year |
| ERP | Enterprise Resource Planning |
| eTOM | enhanced Telecom Operations Map |
| FCE | First-Call Effectiveness |
| FE, BE | Front End, Back End |
| FMCG | Fast Moving Consumer Goods |
| GPS | Global Positioning System |
| GTM | Go-To-Market |
| HCM | Human Capital Management |
| HD | High Definition |
| HR | Human Resources |
| HTML | Hyper-Text Markup Language |
| HTTP | Hyper-Text Transfer Protocol |
| HVAC | Heating, Ventilation, and Air Conditioning |
| IA | Impact Analysis |
| IaaS | Infrastructure-as-a-Service |

| IC | Integrated Circuit |
|---|---|
| ICT | Information and Communication Technology |
| IDI | ICT Development Index |
| IoT | Internet of Things |
| IP | Internet Protocol |
| I-P | Intellectual Property |
| IS | Information Security |
| IT | Information Technology |
| ITU | International Telecommunication Union |
| IVR | Interactive Voice Response |
| JIT | Just-In-Time |
| KPI | Key Performance Indicator |
| KRA | Key Result Area |
| LAN | Local Area Network |
| LED | Light Emitting Diode |
| LOB | Line of Business |
| M2M | Machine-To-Machine |
| MDM | Mobile Device Manager |
| MIS | Management Information Systems |
| MNP | Mobile Number Portability |
| MPLS | Multi-Protocol Label Switching |
| MRI | Magnetic Resonance Imaging |
| MS-DOS | Microsoft Disk Operating System |
| MTBF | Mean Time Between Failures |
| MTTR | Mean Time To Repair |
| MVNO | Mobile Virtual Network Operator |
| NEP | Network Equipment Provider |
| ODC | Offshore Delivery (or Development) Center |
| OEM | Original Equipment Manufacturer |
| OS | Operating System |
| Opex | Operational Expense |
| OTP | One-Time Password |
| OTT | Over the Top |
| P&L | Profit and Loss |
| PaaS | Platform-as-a-Service |

| | |
|---|---|
| PAT | Profit After Tax |
| PB | Peta Bytes |
| PBT | Profit Before Tax |
| PC | Personal Computer |
| PI | Preconceived Idea |
| PO | Purchase Order |
| R&D | Research and Development |
| R&R | Rewards and Recognition |
| RFP | Request For Proposal |
| RIM | Remote Infrastructure Management |
| RM | Release Manager |
| RoI | Return on Investment |
| SA | Solution Architect |
| SaaS | Software-as-a-Service |
| SBU | Strategic Business Unit |
| SC | Solution Consultant |
| SCM | Supply Chain Management |
| SETI | Search for Extra-Terrestrial Intelligence |
| SIM | Subscriber Identity Module |
| SFDC | Salesforce.com |
| SLA | Service Level Agreement |
| SM | Social Media |
| SMAC | Social, Mobility, Analytics, and Cloud |
| SMART | Specific, Measurable, Achievable, Relevant, and Time-bound |
| SME | Small and Medium Enterprises |
| S-M-E | Subject-Matter-Expert |
| SOA | Service Oriented Architecture |
| SR | Service Request |
| SRM | Supplier Relationship Management |
| TA | Tool Administrator |
| TAT | Turn-Around Time |
| TB | Terra Bytes |
| TBO | Think, Build, Operate |
| TCP | Transport Control Protocol |

| TCQ | Time, Cost, Quality |
|------|---------------------|
| TOGAF | The Open Group Architecture Forum |
| TSP | Telecom Service Provider |
| TTM | Time-to-Market |
| UAT | User Acceptance Testing |
| VAS | Value-Added Services |
| VLSI | Very Large-Scale Integration |
| VR | Virtual Reality |
| WAN | Wide Area Network |
| Y2K | Year 2000 |
| Y-o-Y | Year-on-Year |

# Glossary of Terms

| TERM | DEFINITION |
| --- | --- |
| .NET | Microsoft software-application development platform (Windows-based) supporting language interoperability |
| Agile development | a set of methods and practices where solutions evolve through collaboration between cross-functional teams |
| Analog | the opposite of digital. Any technology that doesn't break everything down into binary (digital) code to work is analog |
| Analytics | the discovery, interpretation, and communication of meaningful patterns in data |
| APIs | a set of instructions and standards that allows two software programs to communicate with each other |
| Application server | software that allows development, hosting and rendering of web-based applications to users (clients) |
| Architecture (IT) | the overall design of a computing system's hardware, software, and protocols, and their logical and physical interrelationships |
| Authentication | the process of identifying an individual, based on a user-name and password, or biometric techniques |
| Bandwidth | the amount of data that can be transmitted in a fixed amount of time, or range within a band of frequencies or wavelengths |
| Big Bang | the event at which the Universe came into being and began rapidly expanding from a very high density and temperature state |
| Big data | structured or unstructured data that organizations can potentially mine and analyze for business gains, characterized by high volume, velocity, and variety |
| Big data Analytics | the process of examining large amounts of data to uncover hidden patterns, correlations, and other insights |
| Big Iron | a term used to refer to a mainframe computer |
| BITA Calculator | a simple assessment tool for estimating your BITA score. Also referred as BITA tool |
| Blockchain | a digitized, decentralized, public ledger of all crypto currency (e.g., Bitcoin) transactions |
| C# | a general-purpose, object-oriented programming language developed by Microsoft within its .NET initiative |

| C++, Java | general-purpose, object-oriented programming languages |
|---|---|
| Call Data Record | a record that contains data fields which describe a specific instance of a telecommunication transaction |
| Capex | Capital expense, or funds used by a company to acquire, upgrade, and maintain physical assets |
| Central Processing System | the brain of a computer, which processes all the instructions given to it. Also referred as CPU |
| Churn | a measure of the number of individuals or items moving out of a collective group over a specific period |
| Client | system that rely on servers for processing power |
| Cloud | a distinct IT environment used for remotely delivering computing services—servers, storage, databases, networking, software |
| COBOL | Common Business Oriented Language. English-like computer programming language used for business data processing |
| Compatibility | the capacity for two systems to work together without having to be altered to do so |
| Data center | a facility that centralizes an organization's IT operations and equipment |
| Data Communication Network | an interconnected system of computing devices capable of exchanging digital data amongst them |
| Data mining | the process of sorting through large data sets to identify patterns and establish relationships to solve problems |
| Data science | an interdisciplinary field about scientific methods, processes, and systems to extract knowledge or insights from data |
| Data Visualization | the technique used to convey information by encoding it as visual objects, like patterns and graphs |
| Data Warehouse | central repository constructed by integrating data from multiple heterogeneous sources |
| Data-Processing | the collection and manipulation of items of data to produce meaningful information |
| Digital divide | an inequality relating to access, use, or impact of ICT |
| Digitization | the process of converting information into a digital (computer-readable) format, in which the information is organized into bits |
| e-Commerce | general term for commercial activity over the Internet using B2B, B2C or B2B2C modes |
| Encryption | the process of encoding a message or information in such a way that only authorized parties can access it |
| Engineering | projects delivery unit or organization, e.g., in a software company |

| | |
|---|---|
| Enterprise Mobility | focus on managing mobile devices, wireless networks, and other mobile computing services in a business context |
| Firewall | network security system to monitor and control incoming and outgoing traffic based on predefined rules |
| Gateway | a protocol converter used for linking networks or elements which use different protocols |
| Hadoop | an open-source software framework used for distributed storage and processing of datasets of big data |
| Host | a computer on a network running server and client applications |
| Instant Messaging | online conversations involving real-time exchange of information over the Internet |
| intranet | a private network that is contained within an enterprise |
| IP-based | a system that uses the set of standards which ensure transmission and routing of data packets over the Internet |
| IP-centric | technology shift toward packet-based systems suitable for data communication over the Internet |
| IP-TV | the delivery of television content over Internet Protocol (IP) networks, instead of cable or satellite |
| IPv6 | the most recent version of the Internet Protocol, for identification and location of computers on networks. Replaces IPv4 |
| Iterative development | breaking down the software development of a large application into smaller chunks and repeated cycles |
| Java Enterprise Edition (JEE) | a collection of technologies and APIs for the Java platform designed to support Enterprise Applications |
| JavaScript | programming language of the web—a dynamic programming language for providing interactivity to web pages |
| Line Printer | a machine that prints output from a computer a line at a time rather than character by character |
| Linux | a community-developed Unix-like open source operating system that is supported on most computer platforms |
| Machine learning (ML) | the science of getting computers to act by learning instead of being explicitly programmed to do the task |
| Mainframe | a high-performance computer used for large-scale computing purposes that require greater availability and security |
| Merged reality (MR) | the merging of real and virtual worlds to create visualizations where physical and digital objects coexist and interact |
| Microprocessor | an integrated circuit (IC) which incorporates core functions of a computer's central processing unit (CPU) |

| Minicomputer | a computer that is intermediate between a microcomputer and a mainframe in size, speed, and capacity |
| --- | --- |
| MPLS | (multi-protocol label switching) a data carrying technique for terrestrial high-speed telecommunications networks |
| Multi-factor security | security system that requires more than one form of authentication to verify the legitimacy of a transaction |
| Network | communication fabric for allowing nodes (clients and servers) to share resources |
| Object-oriented | a programming model based on the attributes of objects rather than actions, and data rather than logic |
| Operating System | software that interacts with and manages computer hardware and allows the programs to run |
| Opex | Operational expense, or ongoing cost of running a product, business, or system. |
| Platform (architecture) | the foundation of hardware and software on which enterprise applications are built |
| Plug-and-play | the discovery and use of a hardware component without the need for manual device configuration or user intervention |
| Portal | a website that brings information from diverse sources, like e-mails, online forums and search engines, together seamlessly |
| Real-time | a level of computer (or network) responsiveness that a user senses as instantaneous |
| Relational database | a common type of database whose data is stored in tables and records, as opposed to a flat file |
| Reuse | use of pre-developed blocks of software in current development to optimize development effort |
| Scalability | the capability of a system to handle a growing amount of work, or its potential to be enlarged to accommodate that growth |
| Segmentation | the process of dividing a broad consumer market into subgroups of consumers based on some shared characteristics |
| Server | a centralized processing system that manages, or serves, files, data and applications |
| Shared-service | the provision of a service by one part of the organization to other parts of the organization (like IT or HR services) |
| Silicon | semiconductor material for fabricating Integrated Circuit chips |
| Tape (storage) | data storage medium using spools of magnetic tape which are played on tape drives |
| Telecom | abbreviation for Telecommunications |

| | |
|---|---|
| Time-to-market (TTM) | the length of time it takes from a product being conceived until its being available for sale |
| Tiered data storage | the assignment of different categories of data to various types of storage media to optimize the cost of storage |
| TOGAF | a framework for enterprise architecture that provides an approach for designing, planning, implementing, and governing an enterprise information technology architecture. |
| Transistor | a semiconductor device used to amplify electronic signals |
| Unix | a computer Operating System which is capable of handling activities from multiple users at the same time |
| Virtual machine | an emulation of a computer system, i.e., a computer file, called an image, which behaves like an actual computer |
| Virtualization | the creation of a software-based, or virtual, representation of something (like a server), rather than a physical one |
| Voice-over-IP, VoIP | A technology for the delivery of voice and multimedia sessions over Internet Protocol (IP) networks, such as the Internet |
| Web 2.0 | the next version of the World Wide Web, which emphasizes user-generated content and collaboration |
| Web browser | a software application for retrieving, presenting, and traversing information resources on the World Wide Web |
| Web services | software that makes itself available over the Internet as a service, and uses a standardized messaging system |
| Webserver | Computers that deliver (serve up) web pages. Every web server has an IP address and a domain name |
| World Wide Web | the combination of all resources and users on the Internet that are using the Hypertext Transfer Protocol (HTTP) |
| Y2K | an anticipated computer glitch related to date change from 1999 to 2000 |
| Y-count | total number of Ys (or 1s) in each column (dimension) of BITA calculator |

# Reviews

*Aligning Technology with Business for Digital Transformation* is a practical and useful guide to harnessing the power of Business–Technology alignment, which is an indispensable organizational requirement in this digital era. The book introduces the seven dimensions of alignment—culture, strategy, structure, process, intellect (innovation), function, and tactics—and explores their relevance as the building blocks of personal and enterprise success in the new era. Interspersed with simple and relatable examples, anecdotes, illustrations, tools, and exercises, the book is both interesting and pragmatic, having relevance for students and practitioners from all disciplines.

**Dr. Bimal K. Malaviya**
[Ph. D. Harvard University (Massachusetts Institute of Technology)]. Professor, Aerospace and Nuclear Engineering at Rensselaer Polytechnic Institute, Troy, New York.

Aligning Technology with Business for Digital Transformation is a book with a difference. It is a story of experiences skilfully woven to take you on a journey that would remind of several workplace challenges you dealt with while managing business affairs. Technology is all around and defines our way of life today. Business has become e-business and society has become e-society. We now talk about 5-10G, IoT and Industry 4.0. These are terms beyond sense of integration. It refers to technology entrenched beyond any chance of visualising it as separate entity. With business outcomes being increasingly influenced by information technology (IT), the alignment between Business and IT has become a crucial success factor for an enterprise in this digital age. This book is an intuitive and practical guide to discovering the power of Business–IT alignment and channelling it for personal and organizational growth. The many examples, exercises, and assessment tools in the book make it not only an insightful reference, but also a practical handbook for managing real-world issues. It is an important read for practitioners and students alike.

**Dr. M.P. Gupta**
Head, Department of Management Studies, Indian Institute of Technology, Delhi

Aligning Technology with Business for Digital Transformation is an essential read for everyone who is, or aspires to be, in an organization that relies on technology to meet its business mission. An extract of years of experience with tips, tricks, and practical approaches not found in conventional textbooks and classrooms, it combines the need for Business–IT alignment with the strategic imperatives facing digital enterprises. Business–IT Alignment is an indispensable organizational requirement in the digital era. Read this book to make it work for you as a real business enabler.

**Wg Cdr A.B. Sharma**
Founder and MD, Beyond Evolution Tech Solutions (P) Ltd., Member International Advisory Group (EU) on Trustworthy ICT, Formerly Managing Director at Globacom, Nigeria.

In a world where the very survival of business is dependent on the absorption, assimilation, and effective utilization of digital technology, business and technology are fast becoming indistinguishable from one another. The practical wisdom of this book will help organizations and individuals excel in this new world.

**Amarendra Narayan**
*Former Secretary General, Asia Pacific Telecommunity (APT), Bangkok*

It has indeed been a rewarding experience to have read this book. It very immaculately reintroduces us to concepts that we have always been aware of, but usually set aside for consideration later, in the prioritization between "the Urgent and Important." It is a book that makes one pause and wonder how so much got left to chance! It brings out very articulately the fact that, integrating technology with business is the basic mantra toward building profitable, sustainable, and long-lasting corporations.

**Manoj Verma**

Advisor and Consulting Partner (FMCG - Electrical), Ex CEO, Orient Electric, Ex-President, Consumer Business Unit, Crompton Greaves Ltd, Ex-President ( ELCOMA – Apex Lighting Industry Association ), Ex-Chairman ( IFMA – Indian Fan Manufacturer`s Association )

*The book covers a vital subject without burdening the reader with the complexities of business or the intricacies of technology. The basic concepts talked about in this book remind us of the need to seamlessly intertwine new technology with business basics.*

**Ashim Berry**

Founder/CEO, KMS, Singapore - Leading Business Intelligence and Analytics solution provider in Asia Pacific.

# References

1. Pachory, A. 2019. *Mastering the 7 Dimensions of Business-Technology Alignment*. New York: NY, Business Express Press/Momentum Press.

2. Bill Poole, B. 2018. *Business-IT Alignment—Bill-Poole.blogpost.com*, Creative Abrasion, Perth. Diagrammatic model.

3. The Open Group. 2019. *TOGAF Standard - Version 9.2*. pubs.opengroup.org, Executive Overview.

4. International Telecommunications Union. 2018. *ITU Report on Measuring the Information Society*. ITU Geneva, Executive Overview.

5. SETI@home, (*setiathome.berkeley.edu*, now closed), About SETI@home

6. Samuelson, P.A., and W.D. Nordhaus. 13 July, 2010. *Economics*, 19th ed. McGraw Hill Education.

7. Rob Peterson, R. 2017. *11 Inspiring Cases of Digital Transformation* (biznology.com, 2017), Examples, and Ekaterena Novoseltseva, *Digital Business Transformation: Trends, Statistics and Case Studies*. Apiumhub, Examples.

8. Nichol, P.B. 2018. *Why Enterprise Architecture Maximizes Organizational Value*. IDG Contributor Network, CIO.com, article.

9. Eadicicco, L.M. P., J.P. Pullin, and A. Fitzpatrick. 2017. *The 20 Most Successful Technology Failures of All Time*. TIME Magazine Tech-Innovation, Feature.

10. The Open Group. 2006. *Architecture Principles* (pubs.opengroup.org, 2006), Example set of architecture principles.

# About the Author

**Ashish Pachory** is an Information and Communication Technology (ICT) consultant and leadership guide. In his last appointment, he was the Chief Information Officer (CIO) of the telecom services venture of the Tata group in India. Before joining Tata in 2011, Ashish worked on the other side of the IT/Telecom value chain, in business, operations, and delivery management functions with globally renowned companies like Nokia, Amdocs, Flextronics, Lucent (Bell-Labs), Hughes, and Wipro.

Ashish's work on measuring the business value of IT was recognized among the top IT innovations in 2013 by DynamicCIO (Achievers series). He was conferred Telecom Icon 2013 by Centre of Recognition and Excellence (CORE), and recognized as one of India's most influential Technology Leaders (Economic Times). Also, in 2015, he was recognized among the top 25 global business CIOs by iCMG.

As a thought leader on technology trends and their adoption for business, he has been active as a speaker and panelist at industry forums and has contributed several thought-provoking articles and interviews in various industry and general publications, including the **Economic Times, The Business Standard, Information Week, Voice and Data** and **CIO.com.**

Ashish is a Telecommunications engineer and lives in Gurgaon (INDIA) with his wife, Seema. His interests include astronomy, reading, cryptic crosswords, and cricket.

He invites you to connect on LinkedIn or Twitter (@apachory) to share views and ideas.

# Index

## OTHER TITLES IN THE INFORMATION SYSTEMS COLLECTION

Daniel Power, University of Northern Iowa, Editor

- *Building Successful Information Systems* by Michael Savoie
- *Decision Support, Analytics, and Business Intelligence, Third Edition* by Daniel J. Power and Ciara Heavin
- *Successful ERP Systems* by Jack G Nestell and David L Olson
- *Computer Support for Successful Project Management* by Ulhas Samant
- *Data-Based Decision Making and Digital Transformation* by Daniel J. Power and Ciara Heavin

## Announcing the Business Expert Press Digital Library

*Concise e-books business students need for classroom and research*

This book can also be purchased in an e-book collection by your library as

- a one-time purchase,
- that is owned forever,
- allows for simultaneous readers,
- has no restrictions on printing, and
- can be downloaded as PDFs from within the library community.

Our digital library collections are a great solution to beat the rising cost of textbooks. E-books can be loaded into their course management systems or onto students' e-book readers. The **Business Expert Press** digital libraries are very affordable, with no obligation to buy in future years. For more information, please visit **www.businessexpertpress.com/librarians**. To set up a trial in the United States, please email **sales@businessexpertpress.com**.

www.ingramcontent.com/pod-product-compliance
Lightning Source LLC
Chambersburg PA
CBHW061220220326
41599CB00025B/4708